4/05

BE HEALTHY!

IT'S A GIRL THING:

FOOD, FITNESS, AND FEELING GREAT

LILIAN CHEUNG, D.Sc., R.D., AND MAVIS JUKES

CROWN PUBLISHERS ♛ NEW YORK

Be Healthy! It's a Girl Thing: Food, Fitness, and Feeling Great contains information that has been carefully researched by the authors. It has been reviewed for accuracy by experts in the fields of adolescent psychology, pediatric medicine, and nutrition. This book does not replace your doctor's advice. It is not intended to offer personal medical advice—which should be obtained from a licensed health care provider.

If you have questions about **Be Healthy!,** please discuss them with a parent, physician, pediatrician, registered dietitian, nurse, or other reliable adult.

Published by Crown Publishers, an imprint of Random House Children's Books, a division of Random House, Inc., New York.

CROWN and colophon are trademarks of Random House, Inc.

www.randomhouse.com/kids

Library of Congress Cataloging-in-Publication Data

Jukes, Mavis.

Be healthy! it's a girl thing : food, fitness, and feeling great / Mavis Jukes, Lilian Cheung. — 1st ed.

p.   cm.

Includes index.

Summary: A guide for adolescent girls on how to stay healthy and fit, with information on nutrition and exercise.

ISBN 0-679-89029-7 (trade pbk.) — ISBN 0-679-99029-1 (lib. bdg.)

1. Girls—Health and hygiene—Juvenile literature. 2. Girls—Nutrition—Juvenile literature. 3. Physical fitness for youth—Juvenile literature. [1. Teenage girls—Health and hygiene. 2. Health. 3. Teenage girls—Nutrition. 4. Nutrition. 5. Physical fitness.]

I. Cheung, Lilian. II. Title.

RA777.25.J85 2003   613'.04243—dc21   2003010114

Printed in the United States of America

10 9 8 7 6 5 4 3 2   December 2003

First Edition

For the legendary Marilyn Marlow:
Thank you for who you are, for all you've done.
Love, Mavis

For my parents, my husband, and our sons—thank you.
Love, Lilian

CONTENTS

ACKNOWLEDGMENTS

The authors acknowledge and appreciate those who are dedicating their lives to researching critical issues related to the health and well-being of adolescent girls.

We are especially indebted to the researchers in nutrition and physical activity at the Harvard School of Public Health. We acknowledge the insights and information gained from *Eat Well & Keep Moving* (by Dr. Lilian W. Y. Cheung, Dr. Steven L. Gortmaker, and Hank Dart; Human Kinetics, Inc.) and *Planet Health* (by Jill Carter, Dr. Jean Wiecha, Dr. Karen Peterson, and Dr. Steven L. Gortmaker; Human Kinetics, Inc.).

We thank our colleagues Dr. David Arond, Dr. Bryn Austin, Dr. Patricia Burke, Jill Carter, Dr. Alison Field, Dr. Teresa Fung, Dr. Frank Hu, Dr. Kelly Jackson, Dr. David Ludwig, Kathy McManus, Judy Phillips, Lela Silverstein, Dr. Walter Willett, and Anne Wolf for their critical input. We thank Sandy Gooch, Deborah Keir, and our young reviewers, Hannah Poor, Hannah Williams, Lindsay Williams, Cency Middleton, Alivia Carter, and Amanda Strominger, for their comments. We thank Erin Boyd and Kacey Wardle for their help in the preparation of the manuscript.

SPECIAL THANKS

—For the editing: **Nancy Hinkel**

—For the art direction: **Isabel Warren-Lynch**

—For the book design: **Sarah Hokanson**

—For review in the area of pediatric medicine: **Dr. Sarah Jane Schwarzenberg**

—For review in the area of adolescent psychology: **Dr. Kerri Boutelle**

—For review in the area of adolescent nutrition and lifestyles: **Dr. Mary Story**

ABOUT THIS BOOK

Going through puberty means you're going through a series of dazzling physical, intellectual, and emotional changes called the **growth spurt.**

But it's really not a spurt. It actually takes a few years.

If you're going through puberty, you're in the process of gaining half of your adult bone mass and weight, the last inches of your height, and the ability to reproduce.

At the same time, you're beginning to think more critically. You're acquiring the intellectual and emotional ability to make decisions, including healthy food and lifestyle choices.

AND ALL OF THIS IS HAPPENING AT ONCE!

In order to support this rapid growth, you have very specific needs for food and physical activity.

Be Healthy! It's a Girl Thing: Food, Fitness, and Feeling Great will help you understand the basic information you need to stay healthy and fit.

And feel great.

AND HAVE A GOOD TIME DOING IT

Be Healthy! It's a Girl Thing: Food, Fitness, and Feeling Great gives you the lowdown on how your body uses food; ideas for boosting the nutritional value of what you love to eat, choosing from a fast-food menu, and shopping for food; information on how to link food and physical activity with fun and friendship; and advice on how to think positively and keep your spirits up, how to initiate change by advocating for yourself and friends, and how, when, and where to ask for help when you need it.

DO!

Involve your friends, family, teachers, and health care professionals (physician, pediatrician, nurse, registered dietitian) in evaluating the information in these pages and putting it to work for you in the context of your own cultural traditions, family structure, school environment, economic circumstances, and community.

SOUND GOOD?

Be Healthy! It's a Girl Thing: Food, Fitness, and Feeling Great will help you

- Have more energy

- Improve your ability in sports, exercise, and active games

- Focus and concentrate better in school

- Reduce stress and worries

- Boost your spirits

- Look your best

- Appreciate yourself for who you are

- Counter the negative influence of the media (like TV and magazines) on your food choices—and your self-image

- Work toward getting more nutritious food and more choices for safe, fun physical activity in your school

- Up your chances of being healthy as an adult

- Establish and maintain a beautiful, powerful presence as you move through the world

YOU READY?

chapter 1

C – O – N – N – E – C – T – E – D

Even if you live in the middle of a city and are surrounded by concrete and buildings, you're connected to the earth.

Above your head the moon rises and the sky sizzles with stars, whether you can see them or not.

Below your feet the ground brings forth life in the form of plants—plants that enrich the air you breathe, plants with beautiful, delicate flowers, plants that can fascinate and shade and feed you.

Plants provide food and shelter for animals—animals that gallop or stroll across the land and moo or oink, quack and flap their wings and lay eggs, flip from streams, glide in the sky, ride the tide, cling to the rocks onshore.

You are a 100 percent natural, organic, living being on a planet that can nurture and comfort and energize you—and astound you. Food, physical activity, water, sunshine, and sleep can be balanced to support your healthy growth, peak physical, intellectual, and emotional performance, and a true sense of well-being.

PLANT AND ANIMAL FOODS PROVIDE NUTRIENTS FOR PEOPLE

Nutrients are substances we absolutely, positively must have for energy, growth, and *metabolism*.

Don't let the word **metabolism** throw you. Metabolism is a set of chemical reactions organized in the body that allow you to grow, breathe, have your heart beat, digest food, maintain your body's temperature, and do other things that happen inside you.

1

ENERGY

Your body always, in all ways, uses energy—even when you sleep. In addition to growth and metabolism, it takes energy for your muscles to contract, which is how you move.

SO WHERE DO YOU GET IT?

Only certain nutrients in plant and animal foods have the potential to provide energy: *proteins, carbohydrates,* and *fats.*

NUTRIENT COMBOS

In food, carbohydrates, proteins, and fats appear by themselves or in combination with one another.

An example?

Nuts.

Nuts have all three working for you, along with a laundry list of vitamins and minerals that help your body do its thing.

Vitamins and minerals are also nutrients, but they don't provide energy. Instead, they help your body do stuff that it can't do without them—like form red blood cells and fight infections.

CALORIES

Foods contain different combinations of nutrients and have the possibility (potential) of producing different amounts of energy. The potential is measured in units called *calories.*

EXTRA ENERGY

Extra energy (after meeting your growth and metabolic needs), regardless of whether it's in the protein, carbohydrate, or fat you eat, is stored as body fat. Reserves of energy stored as fat are converted back into usable energy only when you are in an energy-deficit state, that is, burning more calories than you take in.

F.Y.I.

Everybody has body fat and needs it. Fat cells are deposited just under your skin and insulate you from the cold. Fat helps keep your body warm and protects your internal organs; it holds them in place and acts like a cushion.

During puberty in girls, fat tissues increase as part of breast development. Hips and thighs change in size and shape in anticipation of a girl's bearing children someday.

Expect it. It's normal.

BORN TO MOVE

It's primal. Your body is designed to move—to chase animals down into canyons and up hillsides, dig in the ground for roots, reach and stretch to gather berries, plant and harvest seeds, grind grain against rocks, lug around baskets of seeds, climb trees to grab fruit, break sticks and carry wood to build fires for cooking, dance, drum, and play games to celebrate life.

Regardless of your cultural heritage, all families trace back to people who once had to live off the land to survive.

People had to be physically active just to stay alive.

We don't have to hunt and gather our food anymore. We don't have to build a fire to cook. We don't have to walk miles and miles before we can get water to drink.

But we're still human beings who have to move—to stretch our muscles and keep our bodies flexible, to increase our strength, to keep our hearts healthy, to improve our endurance, and to help maintain our *stamina* (ability to perform over time).

F.Y.I.

Movement can improve your posture, help you to feel and look good, and give you more energy. It can help build up your bones, tone your muscles, strengthen your heart, and give your body the practice it needs to master skills to move with grace and coordination: to dance, play music, play sports, play games, do work.

It also can relax you and give you a sense of well-being—and balance.

BALANCE: ENERGY IN, ENERGY OUT

Food reflects the cycle of birth, growth, and renewal of the earth's living things—a cycle that includes you.

What you eat, how much you eat, how often you eat (energy in), how you move, and how often you move (energy out) relate to a 100 percent healthy you.

WATER

Water is a nutrient that drips or drizzles, falls or flutters from the sky onto the ground. It can take the form of mist or steam or fog. It becomes icicles or snow-banks that melt into streams that rush into rivers, collect in lakes. It seeps from springs or is pulled by pumps from wells.

You contain water. In fact, about 70 percent of your body weight is water.

Foods can contain water—and some have lots of it, like watermelon. (Think of it: Raisins are dehydrated, or dried, grapes.)

Among other things, water is needed to regulate your body temperature, carry nutrients around your body, and help get rid of waste.

SUNLIGHT

Sunlight is not only important for building strong bones—it's deeply involved in the process of lifting your spirits.

The sun rises and sets in astounding, flaming shades of orange or pale apricot pastel colors. It warms you and cheers you. It promises that there will always be another tomorrow.

ZZZZZZZZZZZZZZZ

The sun sets for a reason.

Right?

Rest and sleep are essential for good health.

Sleep.

DREAM.

chapter 2

THE ABSOLUTE BASICS ABOUT FOOD

SQUAWK

A hen lays an egg. She sits and sits on it. It hatches into a chick that peeps, pecks bugs and seeds, grows into a hen, and lays an egg.

PLOP

An orange ripens and falls to the ground. It rolls downhill into the sunlight and rots. Its seeds sprout, take root, and grow into trees that produce oranges.

ORANGES AND EGGS

How totally different. But both contain nutrients that your body needs. You can get all the nutrients nature has to offer when you eat a variety of foods from animals and/or plants.

FOODS FROM ANIMALS

POULTRY

Chickens, turkeys, and ducks are **poultry.** Certain wild birds are edible—pheasant, quail, and wild ducks, for example.

EGGS

Edible eggs are laid on a daily basis by cooperative chickens and ducks.

FISH

Fishes that lurk or dart through streams, rivers, and lakes are called **freshwater fish;** perch, catfish, and trout are examples.

Fishes that cruise through the salty water of the ocean are called (you guessed it!) **saltwater fish;** sea bass, tuna, sardines, haddock, cod, and swordfish are examples.

SHELLFISH

Edible shelly critters that live in the oceans include mussels, prawns, shrimp, clams, lobsters, conches, abalone, oysters, and urchins. Octopuses, squids, and eels are also food from the sea.

RED MEAT

Meat from cattle, lamb, deer, elk, rabbits, pigs, and other mammals is called *red meat* because it's red or dark pink before it's cooked.

Organs—heart, kidneys, stomach, etc.—from certain of these animals are called *organ meats*.

DAIRY

Milk or foods that come from the milk of mammals (cows and goats, usually) are called *dairy* foods; butter, cheese, and yogurt are examples because they're all made from milk.

FOODS FROM PLANTS

Plant foods include a bonus along with their nutrients: *fiber*. Foods from animals do not contain fiber.

> ### F.Y.I. FIBER
>
> Fiber supports and strengthens the structure of plants. It holds them up. Fiber is absolutely necessary for humans' healthy digestion. When we eat plant foods, some plant fiber (insoluble) passes right through our system and helps us get rid of waste.
>
> Soluble fiber is fiber that dissolves in water. An example is *pectin,* which is found in fruits and jams. Soluble fiber is heart friendly.

VEGETABLES
STEMS, LEAVES, AND FLOWERS

Asparagus and celery stalks are plant *stems.*

Cabbage, spinach, kale, and lettuce are plant *leaves.*

Cauliflower and broccoli are plant *flowers.*

ROOTS AND TUBERS

Carrots are *roots.* So are turnips, beets, and radishes.

An onion is an edible underground fleshy bud. A potato is a rounded outgrowth of an underground stem (called a *tuber*).

FRUITS

Apples, pears, raspberries, plums, and mangoes—like all fruits and many vegetables—are seed containers.

Fruits are the sweetest ones.

F.Y.I. TRUE COLORS

Deep blue blueberries, bright white cauliflower, intensely orange carrots, brilliant yellow squash, dark green collard greens—foods come in a stunning array of colors. Fruits and vegetables contain chemicals called *phytochemicals*, which help keep your heart healthy and help protect against high blood pressure, stroke, urinary tract infections, and certain diseases, including some kinds of cancer.

This is complex stuff, but let's keep it simple: Eat those fruits and veggies!

NUTS (AND SEEDS)

Nuts are seeds.

Sunflower seeds and pumpkin seeds are examples of other edible seeds.

LEGUMES (AND BEANS)

Seeds in a seed pod that can be split into two sides are **legumes.** Beans like pinto beans, kidney beans, navy beans, lentils, and black beans are legumes. So are peanuts, even though most people think of them as nuts.

Switcheroo: Peanuts become peanut butter! They're still legumes.

GRAINS

The seeds of wheat, rye, oats, brown rice, millet, barley, and corn are **grains.**

Whole grain is grain in its absolutely natural state, which includes the inner *germ layer* and an outer covering called the *bran layer.* (Don't worry—the germ layer doesn't have *germs* in it.)

Whole grains stone-ground into a powdery state is *whole grain flour.* Whole grain flour can be used to make whole grain tortillas, bread, rolls, muffins, pasta, and breakfast cereals.

OILS FROM PLANTS

Avocados, nuts, and seeds contain oils. Plant oils for cooking and dressings can be squeezed from corn, olives, peanuts, soybeans, sunflowers—and other plants.

ALCOHOL

Alcohol is made from grapes, grains, and other plants.

Occasional, very light drinking of alcoholic beverages may have health benefits for some (not all) adults. Regardless, the legal age for drinking alcohol is twenty-one in all states, and alcohol must always be used responsibly. Kids should not drink alcohol.

There's no nutritional advantage that could possibly outweigh the risks of underage drinking—which include being in a drunk-driving accident, using poor judgment that puts you at risk, being physically harmed by another person, getting alcohol poisoning, or getting arrested.

Alcohol poisoning is when there is so much alcohol in someone's system that it interferes with basic body functions. It can cause the person to stagger, fall, throw up, pass out, choke, or stop breathing and die. If you suspect alcohol poisoning, call 911 (or the police emergency number for your area).

WATER AND FLUIDS

Drinking enough water has positive effects on your mood, attention span, and ability to concentrate and to perform physically.

If you don't drink enough fluids, you'll become **dehydrated,** especially when the weather is dry and hot and you are sweating a lot. It's possible to be dehydrated *without* feeling thirsty or hot.

Municipal (city) tap water is fine to drink in the United States—in fact, it may even be better for you than bottled water. City tap water usually contains *fluoride,* a chemical that helps protect your teeth (see page 33).

Set your sights on drinking about six to eight (eight-ounce) cups of fluid (*including water*) over the course of a day (and more if it's very hot out or if you're exercising vigorously). Drink before, during, and after long periods of physical activity. Even if it's winter! But don't drink too much at one time!

How do you know if you are drinking enough? One way is to check out the color of your urine (pee). It should be pale yellow, practically clear—not deep yellow or orange. See page 31 for more on fluid intake.

HEADS UP!

You can become very dehydrated during long periods of strenuous physical activity—especially when it's hot out. Fluids that contain sugar and salts (sports drinks)—not just tap water—should be drunk to replenish lost salts and provide a short-term boost in energy if you are exercising strenuously in the heat. Very hot out? Wait till it cools down to exercise strenuously!

SUNSHINE

Your body needs about fifteen minutes a day of sunlight on your face and hands for your skin to make vitamin D, which is needed to build strong bones.

But please use common sense: You're not supposed to fry yourself. Wear sun-block (and a hat) if you plan to be outside in the sun for extended periods.

SPF stands for Sun Protectant Factor. Why not go for the strong stuff: SPF 30 or above. But there are limits to the effectiveness of sunscreen, so you may also need to cover up or find shade. Unprotected exposure to the sun's rays can cause damaging sunburns, which may contribute to developing **melanoma** (cancer of the skin pigment) and premature aging of the skin (wrinkles) later on in life.

YOU KNOW YOU CAN—

Drink water, let the sun shine on you. It's a cinch!

You can also figure out how to have fun with physical activity—you really can!

Understanding the basics of how food works isn't as complicated as it seems—it's not!

You can do this. You already know more than you think!

All you need is a plan, and we can help you.

YOU IN?

chapter 3

HOW FOOD WORKS

DIGESTING FOOD (BURP)

Here's the basic lowdown on how food works for you:

Cells are the building blocks of every single living organism on earth, including us. They're tiny little structures so small, you need a microscope to look at 'em. Cells are called building blocks, but a cell isn't a block and it's not solid.

So go figure.

We have millions of living cells within us, and every one of them needs a very precise form of energy in order to function.

The energy is provided by carbohydrates (carbs), proteins, and fats in the food we eat and drink. During *digestion,* the structure of proteins, fats, and carbs is broken down, down, down into very tiny, usable pieces, which are carried through our blood to cells.

Each cell is like an incredibly complex little factory that has a specific job to complete for the good of our whole body.

THE MACROS (AKA MACRONUTRIENTS)

Proteins, carbohydrates, and fats are called **macronutrients** (big nutrients). We need lots of these. They're our only source of energy.

Foods contain a variety of different nutrients. Some foods are famous for their high protein content (fish and chicken, for example), others are famous for their high carb content (cereals and rice), and others are famous for their fat content (olive oil and nuts).

CARBOHYDRATES (CARBS)

"Carbs" is the family name for sugars and starches.

Once we chew up or drink food containing carbs, our body immediately gets to business breaking them down into their basic building block—*glucose*—and uses glucose for energy.

Carbs make natural appearances in everything from bananas to grains to milk. But carbohydrates are also **added** to some of the foods we eat and drink; white sugar, brown sugar, honey, molasses, and corn syrup are all carbs commonly used to sweeten food. These carbs are **simple sugars.** They're quickly changed to glucose, giving you a fast burst of energy.

Carbs in certain other foods—low-fat (1 percent) milk, for example—are broken down into glucose more gradually, giving you energy over a longer period of time.

Foods high in added sugar, like soft drinks, do provide quick energy—but often don't contain other macronutrients or vitamin and mineral perks.

PROTEIN

Your body is capable of converting protein into glucose and using it for energy (or storing it) if it wants to—but protein is more about growth and repair of cells.

Just about every food has protein in it—except sugar and fats (like butter and oil).

During digestion, proteins are broken down into their simplest building blocks (*amino acids*) and reassembled in various ways. (Think Legos here.) Your body can produce some, but not all, of its own amino acids. The **essential** amino acids are the ones you have to get in food because your body can't produce them.

Animal foods are particularly rich sources of protein—and are called *complete proteins* because they contain all the essential amino acids your body requires. It's also possible to get all the essential amino acids from plant-based foods when you eat the right combination of legumes (beans), whole grains, and nuts (see page 54).

F.Y.I.

Protein supplements do **not** build muscle mass. Working out builds muscle mass. Please don't buy or use these products.

FATS

Fats really deliver energy, especially in the long run. They're so energy-rich that they have more than twice as many calories per gram as carbs and proteins.

Fats give flavor and texture to food. And they keep you from feeling too hungry. They're absolutely necessary for carting around specific fat-soluble vitamins (A, D, E, and K). And they keep your skin smooth.

Both plant and animal foods contain fats.

Certain plant foods, like nuts, avocados, seeds, and plant oils—and also certain fish, like salmon—contain fats that really do extremely good things for your heart. See page 23.

THE MINIS (AKA MICRONUTRIENTS)

Vitamins and minerals don't provide energy—they help your body do stuff.

We need only tiny amounts of vitamins and minerals. That's why these nutrients are called *micronutrients*. (*Micro* basically means *mini*.)

With guidance from research scientists, the Food and Nutrition Board of the National Academy of Sciences has established how much we need of each vitamin and mineral.

You *can* get all the vitamins and minerals you need by following a healthy eating plan that includes a wide variety of foods (see page 25).

But some vitamins and minerals can be hard to scout out in food—especially for busy people who eat and snack on the run. So certain key vitamins and minerals are routinely added to some foods to make sure the general population gets enough of them. Foods with added nutrients are called "enriched" or "fortified." Milk, juice, bread, cereal, pasta, and other grain foods are commonly fortified/enriched. (Check the ingredients label on the packaging.)

IF YOUR DOCTOR RECOMMENDS IT...

...you can take one daily (complete) multi-vitamin/multimineral supplement for kids as a nutritional backup. **But it won't make up for an unhealthy eating pattern.**

Only **one** should be taken each day. It should be taken after a meal. Fat from food is needed for certain vitamins (fat-soluble) to be absorbed in your body (see page 13).

Fat-soluble vitamins accumulate in the body and build up: like vitamins A and D. Chronically high doses of certain vitamins are toxic. Please do NOT take more than one daily (complete) multivitamin/multimineral supplement for kids and please do NOT take doses of single vitamins or minerals separately —unless prescribed by your doctor.

If you have young children in the house, make sure the bottle has a childproof cap. And keep the supplements out of their reach. They contain iron. Accidental over-dose of products containing iron is the leading cause of **fatal** (causing death) poisoning in children under age six. FYI: Poison Control Hotline, **1–800–222–1222.** Call free, day or night, anywhere in the United States.

For more about the function and sources of vitamins and minerals, see pages 110 to 112.

KEY VITAMINS FOR THE GROWTH SPURT

B VITAMINS

B vitamins (B-1, B-2, B-3, B-6, and B-12) are needed for converting food into energy; healthy eyes, skin, muscles, and red blood cells; and having a healthy nervous system. Good sources of B vitamins are leafy green vegetables, milk (1 percent low-fat or skim), legumes, nuts, seeds, whole grains, eggs, and chicken.

FOLIC ACID

It's a good idea to get into the habit of routinely eating foods that are rich in folic acid since it reduces your heart disease and cancer risks. Folic acid is a vitamin that has special importance to women of childbearing age. Good sources include dark green leafy vegetables (like spinach and romaine lettuce), fruits (like oranges), dried beans, whole grain breads, and enriched grain products like fortified cereals. (For more sources, see page 111.)

Too little folic acid in pregnancy causes birth defects. So women are advised to take *folate* for a few months in advance of becoming pregnant. Some (not all) doctors recommend that girls who have reached puberty take a daily (complete) multivitamin/multimineral supplement for kids, which contains folic acid. Ask your doctor if he or she recommends this for you.

VITAMIN D

Vitamin D and calcium work together in the bone-building process. Our skin makes vitamin D when exposed to the sun. But to *make sure* we get enough vitamin D, it's added to milk. Fortified breakfast cereals have vitamin D *and* calcium added. Check out food labels (see page 72).

AH! BUT WHAT IF YOU DON'T DRINK MILK?

Vitamin D can also be found in salmon, egg yolk, fortified cereals, and fortified soy milk (and in daily [complete] multivitamin/multimineral supplements for kids).

KEY MINERALS FOR THE GROWTH SPURT

What's up with minerals is that they help our blood carry oxygen and nutrients to muscles and other body parts and help build strong teeth and bones—as well as performing other wonderful benefits for our health.

Two really important minerals for girls are *calcium* and *iron*.

CALCIUM

Calcium is absolutely essential for reaching your genetic potential (all you are programmed to be) for height and building strong bones.

And your bones are growing like crazy right now!

Seize the moment! Never again will you have this same opportunity and time span to increase your bone mass, ever! If you miss this window of opportunity, you may become vulnerable to your bones thinning later in life (*osteoporosis*).

> **F.Y.I.**
>
> **Weight-bearing exercise,** during which your bones carry the weight of your body or other weight—like walking or playing volleyball or basketball—is also a big factor in keeping your bones strong.

Calcium is found in dairy products (like 1 percent low-fat or skim milk, yogurt, and cheese), canned sardines and canned salmon, spinach, and certain dark green leafy vegetables like collard greens, bok choy, turnip greens, mustard greens, and kale. Broccoli and carrots also contain it.

Tempeh (like cheese but made with beans and/or grains), white beans, soybeans, and soy nuts all contain calcium.

Foods fortified with calcium include fortified orange juice, soy milk, soy yogurt, soy cheese, and firm tofu (made with calcium sulfate). Enriched breakfast cereals and certain enriched breads have added calcium.

You can also hunt calcium down in almonds, molasses, and canned pinto beans (and in daily [complete] multivitamin/multimineral supplements for kids).

GOT MILK? (SKIM OR 1 PERCENT, THAT IS)

Your bones want and need the calcium and vitamin D present in milk. Your body likes the quantities of protein, carbohydrate, and other nutrients present in milk. Whole milk has too much heart-unfriendly *saturated fat* (see page 23) to drink on a routine basis. That is why 1 percent low-fat or skim milk is the way to go: The saturated fat has been removed, but the other nutrients remain the same!

However: Most little peeps age two and under are advised to drink higher-fat milk. Ask the pediatrician.

LACTOSE INTOLERANCE

Some of us don't produce enough of the enzyme **lactase,** which helps break down the sugar **(lactose)** found in dairy foods (and certain other foods; see below).

Do you have gas, bloating, cramps, and/or diarrhea after eating dairy foods or drinking milk? If so, you **may** be lactose intolerant. How do you know for sure?

Your health care professional can help you determine this.

Tips for getting enough calcium if you are lactose intolerant (or prefer to avoid milk):

1. Eat broccoli, collard greens, kale, turnip greens, mustard greens, and bok choy: good sources of calcium.

2. Calcium-fortified soy products (soy milk, tofu, and soy yogurt) are nondairy sources of calcium.

3. Calcium-fortified juices and cereals are also available.

Ask your health care professional if he or she recommends that you take a calcium supplement. Or maybe he or she will suggest that you add a little extra lactase to your meals. Lactase can be purchased without a prescription. It comes in liquid, chewable, or capsule form. **If your health care professional recommends it,** take a lactase tablet before drinking milk or eating other dairy products, add lactase drops to milk—or buy milk that has been treated with the enzyme.

F.Y.I.

NONDAIRY FOODS SOMETIMES CONTAIN LACTOSE

Some breads, breakfast drinks, margarines, snack foods, pancake mixes, and baked goods may contain "hidden" lactose. Check the labels.

IRON

Going through puberty means your reproductive system has begun to function. Or is soon about to.

Iron is a mineral that's **especially** important for girls because of *menstruation* (having your period).

Beginning to have periods means that your reproductive system has begun to function. The tiny eggs contained in your two reproductive organs (called **ovaries**) have begun to mature. Your period can start anytime between about the ages of nine and sixteen.

When you're having a period, which lasts a few days, a small amount of bloody fluid trickles out of your body. Just a certain, predetermined amount of blood is released. Then it stops.

It may take one to two years to "regularize," but once it starts, most girls have a period once a month until the age of about fifty. That's when having periods stops **(menopause).**

HOW THIS RELATES

Iron is part of a compound in your blood (*hemoglobin*) that carries oxygen to every cell of the body. When blood is lost through having your period each month, the iron has to be replaced. Your body needs the raw material (iron) to re-create hemoglobin.

But your body can't make iron for itself. When you're not getting enough iron, you feel tired—lacking in energy.

Cooked dry beans—like black beans, kidney beans, and pinto beans—contain iron. Chickpeas (garbanzo beans), lentils, soybeans, seeds, firm tofu, and certain dark vegetables—like spinach, collard greens, and kale—all contain iron.

Lean red meat (especially beef) is a good source of iron. It's also in shellfish, sardines, and dark turkey meat. And there are other good sources, such as iron-fortified breads and cereals (and in daily [complete] multivitamin/multimineral supplements for kids).

ZZZZZZZZ

Getting plenty of sleep—and still feel groggy? Nodding off in class? Talk to your pediatrician.

Many, many teen girls are short on iron.

Besides fatigue (being tired), not enough iron (called *iron deficiency*) causes shortened attention span. It gets in the way of your intellectual performance, reduces your body's ability to fight off infections, and makes you less able to do work.

A NOTE ON SODIUM

Hey. While we're talking minerals, salt (which contains sodium) may add zest and life to certain foods—but your body doesn't like too much of it!

So please pass the saltshaker . . . right on past you. Or at least limit the sprinkling! The unique flavors of food will make themselves known to you once they're not overpowered by salt.

F.Y.I.—SOME SALTY SIDEWINDERS

Don't overdo these foods. Easy does it with:

1. Canned soup and soup that comes in packages (unless low sodium)

2. Canned gravy

3. Beef jerky

4. Bacon bits

5. Table salt

6. Dill pickles

7. Teriyaki sauce

8. Cured ham

9. Soy sauce

10. Processed "cheese food"

11. Salty chips

12. Pepperoni

13. Hot dogs

14. Bacon

Also: Sodium is used as a preservative (*sodium nitrate*) and flavor enhancer (*monosodium glutamate*—MSG) in many highly processed foods like soups, salad dressings, and frozen dinners.

HERBAL MEDICINES AND HERBAL SUPPLEMENTS

Certain herbs and/or plant parts contain strong natural chemicals.

At the time of publication of this book, standards regulating the sale of herbs and the products that contain them aren't completely in place.

Until standards are fully developed, it will be hard to know for sure whether a certain product is pure, what it's actually made of, how strong it is, whether it works, and what side effects it may have.

It will also be hard to know if claims made by the people who sell the product are sci-entifically based or, in some cases, whether it's even safe to use.

Combining drugs (including natural chemicals) can potentially cause dangerous reactions. Herbal medications and/or herbal supplements may interfere with prescription medication you may be taking or even complicate an existing medical condition.

Before taking an herbal medication or herbal supplement, please run it past your pharmacist or another health care professional.

NUTRITION ON THE NET

BE HEALTHY! IT'S A GIRL THING: FOOD, FITNESS, AND FEELING GREAT recommends the following reliable Web sites on nutrition, health, and fitness.

THE CENTER FOR YOUNG WOMEN'S HEALTH

http://www.youngwomenshealth.org

CENTERS FOR DISEASE CONTROL (CDC) BAM! BODY AND MIND

http://www.bam.gov

POWERFUL BONES. POWERFUL GIRLS.

http://www.cdc.gov/powerfulbones

NUTRITION & PHYSICAL ACTIVITY

http://www.cdc.gov/nccdphp/dnpa/ bonehealth/bonehealth.htm

FOOD AND DRUG ADMINISTRATION KIDS' HOME PAGE

http://www.fda.gov/oc/opacom/kids

HEALTH AND HUMAN SERVICES HEALTHFINDER AND PAGES FOR KIDS

http://www.healthfinder.gov/kids

http://www.hhs.gov/kids

HARVARD SCHOOL OF PUBLIC HEALTH'S NUTRITION SOURCE

http://www.hsph.harvard.edu/nutritionsource

NUTRITION NAVIGATOR: A RATING GUIDE TO NUTRITION WEBSITES

http://www.navigator.tufts.edu

PRODUCE MARKETING ASSOCIATION AND PRODUCE FOR BETTER HEALTH FOUNDATION

http://www.aboutproduce.com

TAKE CHARGE OF YOUR HEALTH: A TEENAGER'S GUIDE TO BETTER HEALTH

http://www.niddk.nih.gov/
health/nutrit/pubs/winteen

If you want additional info about health, nutrition, and fitness on the Internet, work with your parent and keep the following guidelines in mind:

CHECKING OUT INTERNET HEALTH / MEDICAL RESOURCES

The question is:

Is the site trustworthy?

It doesn't take much more than some basic computer literacy to set up a site. How do you make sure that information on the Web about nutrition, fitness, and other health issues is reliable?

Tip list (*adapted from United Health Foundation*):

1. Visit four to six sites so that you can get a full picture of the information you want.

2. Investigate: Who runs the site? If it's a good one, the people running it will be the first to say who's responsible for the information. Credibility and credentials (proper training and proof of it) of the Web site publisher are absolutely key.

3. Who wrote the ACTUAL information? Information on nutrition should be provided by a qualified professional—that is, a registered dietitian, doctor, or professor of nutrition at an established educational institution or government agency, and their credentials should be easy to find on the site.

4. What is the source of the information? Did the person create it or borrow it from another site?

5. Check the date to make sure the information is current. Information on health is continually changing.

6. Is there a scientific basis for the information—or are we talking about gut feelings and anecdotes (personal stories and/or testimonies) being passed along? These aren't reliable.

7. What is the purpose of the site? It should include a "mission statement"—or "About this site"—that includes its purpose.

8. Is somebody trying to sell you something? The sites you rely on should be well established or else run by the government—and not set up for commercial purposes.

9. Don't give out any personal information about yourself to an Internet site without your parent working with you. And even with your parent involved, be sure why you are being asked for personal information about yourself before giving it.

10. Share the information gathered with your health care professional and make sure he or she is aware of the sources for it.

HEADS UP!

Things aren't always what they seem.

Sorry, but yes—creepy adults posing as kids on the Internet **are** a definite threat.

You wouldn't strike up a conversation with a stranger in the mall, so don't chat it up in chat rooms. You don't want any sleazeballs showing up!

THE REAL DEAL

Communication with real people that you know and trust or meet under safe, age-appropriate circumstances is the way to build strong, healthy relationships and expand your circle of friends.

DO THAT.

chapter 4

WHAT IT IS

Your heart is a beautiful, powerful little pump made of muscle that pumps and pumps.

And pumps.

Think of it: Some hearts pump nonstop for over a hundred years.

Your heart pushes blood throughout your body in tubes called **blood vessels: veins** and **arteries.** Blood vessels are flexible so they can accommodate the different levels of pressure that occur as your heart beats and pushes blood through them.

THE HEART-LUNG CONNECTION

You have two lungs, and it's their job to deliver *oxygen* into your bloodstream. Oxygen is present throughout nature, in combination with other elements. It's in the air you breathe.

Your lungs have **quite** a job—considering that oxygen is required by every cell in your body. All tissues in our body need to have oxygen delivered to them or they will die.

> **F.Y.I.**
>
> Your lungs need to remain healthy and strong in order to deliver oxygen to your blood. Smoking damages the lungs. Every year, 400,000 Americans die as a result of tobacco-related illneses, including lung disease, heart disease, and cancer.

In order for blood to deliver oxygen and other essentials to cells throughout the body, it must be able to pass freely through vessels that are open and flexible. Over time, eating too much saturated and *trans* fats (see page 23) can increase a person's risk of developing arteries that are narrow, hard, clogged—or even completely blocked. This is *cardiovascular disease,* and it can have serious consequences, including a heart attack or stroke.

HEART-FRIENDLY FATS (UNSATURATED FATS)

There are certain fats (oils) your heart just **l-o-v-e** loves!

Fats from certain fish are very heart friendly! Fats in salmon and saltwater fish like tuna, sardines, and herring keep the inside walls of your arteries open and flexible.

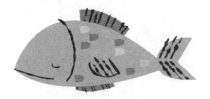

Almost all oils from plants are heart helpers (olive, corn, soybean, canola, sunflower, peanut). But two tropical plant oils—palm and coconut—and vegetable oils that have been chemically altered (*trans* fat) are not.

FATS NOT FRIENDLY TO THE HEART (*TRANS* FATS AND SATURATED FATS)

1. Someone has been fiddling around with plant oils in the lab: Trans fats (trans-fatty acids)

Vegetable shortening and stick margarine are plant oils that have been chemically altered: *hydrogenated*. Ah! Hahahaha!

Their very structure has been changed! They are **solid** at room temperature instead of **liquid.** This process makes perfectly heart-friendly plant oils into the frightful stuff called trans fat.

> ### F.Y.I. HEART-FRIENDLY MARGARINE
> Margarines that list **un**saturated and **un**hydrogenated liquids or vegetable oils as their first ingredient are friendly to the heart. Choose soft tub margarines, liquid margarines, and/or vegetable spreads. (Most of these will be labeled "No trans fat.")

Trans fat increases the risk of getting heart disease when you're a grownie. Trans fat is also known as *hydrogenated oil* and *partially hydrogenated oil*.

2. Saturated fats

Saturated fats are found in palm and coconut oil, trans fats, and certain animal foods, like butter, whole milk, and red meat. Saturated fats can contribute to clogging up your arteries.

Limiting foods made with hydrogenated oils; cooking with unhydrogenated plant oils (not including palm or coconut) instead of butter, lard, or shortening; trimming fat from meat; and removing skin from poultry help you cut down on saturated fat.

Thinking of beef, pork, and lamb as occasional foods rather than everyday foods and using butter sparingly are two more steps in the right direction (see pages 36 to 37).

3. Cholesterol

Cholesterol is produced by the liver, and it's also present in certain animal foods that we eat. Plant foods don't contain any cholesterol; only animal foods do.

Eating too much saturated fat over time may be associated with high cholesterol levels in the blood—which is associated with increased risk of heart disease.

Your body **does** need cholesterol but can manufacture enough of its own. It doesn't require extra from your diet.

One of the reasons we suggest varying your choices in the LEAN ANIMAL PROTEIN group (see page 36) is that egg yolks are relatively high in cholesterol. Try not to eat more than 3 egg yolks a week.

HEADS UP! SMOKING AND YOUR ARTERIES

Hey! The tobacco companies forgot to tell us (oops!) a few minor details about stuff related to tobacco that can kill us—including this:

Nicotine, carbon monoxide, and other dangerous substances in cigarette smoke damage the walls of your arteries—including the arteries that bring oxygen and nutrients to your heart.

Now why would anyone want to deprive such a beautiful, hardworking, faithful heart muscle of the things it needs?

And P.S. Remember: That faithful little muscle especially loves fruits and vegetables loaded with fiber and chemicals that help prevent heart disease (and cancer).

So let's hear it for:

Apples, bananas, blackberries, blueberries, Brussels sprouts, carrots, cherries, cooked beans and peas, dates, figs, grapefruit, kiwi fruit, oranges, pears, prunes, raspberries, spinach, strawberries, sweet potatoes, and tomatoes.

YAY!

chapter **5**

MAINTAINING THE BALANCE: THE CACTUS PLAN

Okay. So the amounts and types of food that you eat and drink need to be in balance with the energy your body uses for growing, moving, and performing its metabolic functions— like breathing and digestion.

?

But how **do** you balance these things?

GREAT NEWS!

Most of this balance involves doing what comes naturally; it's a blast to romp and play games and sports, refreshing to glug down cool water, satisfying to chomp into fresh, crisp fruits and vegetables, fun to munch snacks or have lunch with a bunch of friends, comforting to sit down to yummy home-cooked family dinners, and (yawn) lovely to snuggle

    deep

    down

into your covers

for a good night's sleep.

So you already know a lot.

STILL, THERE'S A TON OF INFORMATION OUT THERE— AND ORGANIZING IT IS KEY.

A cactus might seem like an unusual graphic to use for a food and physical activity guideline. That's because . . . **IT IS UNUSUAL!**

INTRODUCING: TA–DA!

THE CACTUS PLAN

WE'LL WALK YOU THROUGH IT. BUT DO UNDERSTAND THAT EVERYTHING TO DO WITH THE CACTUS PLAN IS FURTHER EXPLAINED IN THE TEXT OF THIS BOOK.

The Cactus Plan is food and physical activity guidelines basically represented by a (labeled) drawing of a cactus, a sun, a moon—and a rainbow.

    The drawing of this cactus, sunning itself

under the sun, dozing under the moon, and sitting within view of a rainbow, can loosely represent you: also an organic being on planet Earth.

The Cactus Plan describes, in pictures, words, and numbers, one very good strategy for staying hydrated (having enough fluid on board), nourishing your body, sustaining your energy, keeping your energy (calorie) intake in balance with your activity level, and feeling emotionally strong by staying connected with people you love and trust—and asking for help when you need it.

> ## F.Y.I.
>
> The future health of your heart and body is also carefully considered and built into The Cactus Plan, along with enhancing your chances of avoiding certain common chronic (ongoing) illnesses (like type 2 diabetes) when you are an adult or older teen.

THE FOOD GROUPS

Related foods are grouped together and represented within separate sections of the cactus.

The drawing includes the approximate amount of servings you should try to eat each day from each group. (Serving sizes are explained in the following chapter.)

ENERGY INTAKE

If you follow The Cactus Plan, you'll be drinking plenty of fluids. You'll be eating three nutritious meals a day: breakfast, lunch, and dinner, and two healthy snacks.

This will ensure that you are getting enough nutrients and energy (calories) to support your metabolism, achieve your potential for growth (including height), intellectual performance, and emotional well-being, and fuel your body for physical activity (about 2,000–2,200 calories a day).

But you may need to eat and drink more if you're very physically active—or if your health care professional advises adjustments to meet your individual needs.

YES, WE'VE ALL HAD DAYS . . .

. . . And may have more days when we, say, skip lunch and snack on chips.

Establishing and maintaining a healthy eating and activity pattern **over the long run** is what The Cactus Plan is all about. So please think of it as a general guideline, not as something that has to be followed to the letter every day of your life.

But **do** think of it. It can really help you make healthy food and physical activity choices right now—when good nutrition and routine activity are so important for your physical, emotional, and intellectual (brain power) growth.

THE BASIC CONCEPT

The basic concept behind The Cactus Plan is this:

It's very healthy to fill up on a variety of nutrient-rich plant foods: whole grains, colorful fruits and vegetables, nuts, and beans (and other legumes). And to use oils from plants for dressings and in cooking. Why? Because plants have heart-helping fats, fiber, and those chemicals that can help prevent diseases (*phytochemicals;* see page 7).

But even though we're emphasizing eating lots of plant foods, The Cactus Plan allows us plenty of servings of a variety of nutrient-rich animal foods: 1 percent low-fat and skim milk, low-fat or nonfat yogurt and low-fat or nonfat cheese, and poultry, fish, seafood, eggs, and lean red meat.

BUT PUL–EESE! NOTE

The Cactus Plan, in honor of long-term health considerations, recommends that you vary your choices in the LEAN ANIMAL PROTEIN group. Eggs and lean red meat should be eaten in moderation. Also, there are suggested limits on how much and how often we should eat certain specific fish because of possible mercury contamination. Do read and follow government guidelines posted in your grocery store and/or on food packaging.

Questions? Call the U.S. Food and Drug Administration Center for Food Safety and Applied Nutrition information line: **1–888–SAFEFOOD.** Or call your local health department to find out what fish should be limited.

CALLING ALL VEGETARIANS!

If you don't eat animal foods, be sure to talk to a doctor or registered dietitian about appropriate plant substitutions for animal foods, how to **combine** these substitutions effectively so that you get enough of the right kinds of nutrients, and whether or not you should take calcium supplements.

The same goes if you can't tolerate dairy foods and other foods with lactose in them. Your doctor can help you come up with a strategy to make sure you get enough calcium. Lactose intolerance and vegetarian plans are explained in chapters 3 and 9 of this book.

OCCASIONAL FOODS

Foods noted as "occasional" foods in the cactus key are represented as sections of cactus with prickles on the ends.

The plan isn't suggesting that you don't eat or drink these.

Do eat them and drink them occasionally, if you like.

But e-a-s-y does it!

Limit your portion size.

Don't go overboard.

ENERGY OUTPUT

We know, we know. Cactuses just sit there. They don't jump rope or do jumping jacks. But they **do** grow.

Routine physical activity recommendations are represented on the right side of the cactus plant—and thoroughly explained in chapters 13 and 14.

If you have a physical condition that prevents you from exercising normally, don't be discouraged. But **do** talk to your doctor before beginning or changing your exercise program.

That way, you can work together to tailor a plan that's safe and effective for you.

Recommendations for physical activity may vary according to a girl's age. Recommendations for energy intake can vary according to a girl's age, size, physical activity levels, and what stage of puberty she's in. The Cactus Plan is meant to give general guidelines. To reflect this, there is a range in regard to numbers of servings of foods, energy intake, and physical activity. Specific questions? Run them past your own health care professional.

OTHER ELEMENTS

Sleeping enough, letting the sun (gently) shine on your face and hands for about fifteen minutes every day, and taking one daily (complete) multivitamin/multimineral supplement for kids as a backup (if your doctor recommends this) are also elements of the plan.

And so is the rainbow, representing the positive feelings that result from maintaining strong communication with your family, friends, teachers, medical professionals, and other trustworthy, responsible adults—and asking for help when you need it.

Open to enjoying every food there is under the sun—in amounts your body can put to work optimally?

READ ON.

The Cactus Plan

Communicate with your friends, family, health care professionals, teachers, and/or other responsible adults and ask for help when you need it.

Sleep 8 hours every night.

15 minutes total of mild sunshine on your face and hands every day (but don't "tan")

LACTOSE INTOLERANT? DON'T EAT ANIMAL FOODS?
Talk to your doctor or a registered dietitian about making appropriate substitutions and/or taking vitamins and/or mineral supplements.

LIMIT fatty, processed meats, like bacon, sausage, and salami.

LEAN ANIMAL PROTEIN
poultry, fish and other seafood, eggs, lean red meat, 1-2 servings a day Vary your choices. (Don't choose red meat *every* day.)

CACTUS KEY

——— **LIMIT THESE**
Think: Occasionally!

LIMIT butter and ice cream.

LOW-FAT DAIRY FOODS
low-fat milk, low-fat yogurt, low-fat cheese, 3 servings a day

LIMIT hydrogenated oil (*trans* fat), coconut oil, and palm oil.

LIMIT TV and screen time to 2 hours a day, max.

Use **PLANT OILS** every day for cooking and dressings. About 3 tablespoons total.

NUTS AND BEANS (AND OTHER LEGUMES)
including tofu and other soy protein foods, 1 to 2 servings a day

LIMIT white potatoes and french fries.

SUSTAINED PHYSICAL ACTIVITY
3 days or more a week, about 15–20 minutes of your hour (see below) should be sustained activity. During this time, you should alternate moderate to vigorous exercise with brief periods of rest and recovery.

HEALTH CONCERNS REGARDING EXERCISING?
Talk to your doctor about making an exercise plan just for you.

VEGETABLES
Eat lots and lots. 4 servings a day

FRUITS
3 servings every day

ACCUMULATED (ADDED UP OVER THE DAY) MODERATE PHYSICAL ACTIVITY
Your daily moderate physical activity should add up to a total of at least 1 hour or more each day. (See above.)

LIMIT refined sugary cereals, white bread, white pasta, white rice.

GRAINS
about 6–8 servings a day (mostly whole grains)

LIMIT candy.

LIMIT drinks with added sugar.

LIMIT sugary baked goods like cakes, cookies, and doughnuts.

FLUIDS
Drink a total of 6–8 (8-ounce) cups of fluids (including water) over the course of every day.

Eat 3 nutritious meals—breakfast, lunch, and dinner—and 2 healthy snacks every day.

Balance **ENERGY INPUT** → (calories you take in from food and fluids—about 2,000–2,200 calories a day, and more if you're very physically active)

with →

ENERGY OUTPUT (routine physical activity—plus growth and metabolism, which happen on their own)

chapter **6**

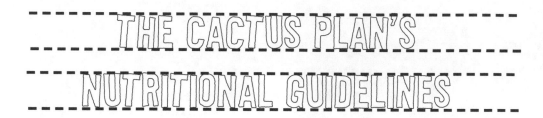

THE CACTUS PLAN'S NUTRITIONAL GUIDELINES

Nutritional guidelines aren't strict rules. They're suggestions that can lead you into a healthy eating pattern.

If you don't score enough servings from every group represented on the cactus every day, that's fine.

SERVING SIZES

There's a key to understanding the concept of serving sizes: Guesstimate.

(Yes, guess!)

GUESSTIMATING TIPS
A SERVING IS DIFFERENT FROM A HELPING AND/OR A PORTION

A helping/portion (like half a barbecued chicken) may actually count for two or three servings of poultry.

A great big, crispy salad with ruffly lettuce, cherry tomatoes, onions, green peppers, and carrots may count as two or three servings of vegetables.

A turkey sandwich with lettuce, sliced tomatoes, and low-fat cheese, a bowl of beef vegetable soup, a carne asada burrito, pasta primavera, falafel, chicken chow mein—all of these are combo foods and count as servings but in different groups.

You **really** have to guesstimate with combo foods!

AND ANYWAY!

How do you accurately measure a cup of something that can't fit into a cup? You can't. So don't. And don't stress about it.

HOCKEY PUCK, DECK OF CARDS, TENNIS BALL, AND A TUBE OF LIPSTICK?

Familiar objects? These can help give you a general idea about serving sizes.

LET'S BEGIN WITH FLUIDS

Fluids are liquids. The recommended total daily amount of fluids for girls your age is about six to eight (eight-ounce) cups *spaced over the course of a day*. Your fluid intake should include water. Why not keep a pitcher full in your fridge with slices of lemon in it?

DOES SIX TO EIGHT CUPS SEEM LIKE A LOT?

Remember: Everything counts toward the total.

Soups, juice, juice bars, 1 percent low-fat or skim milk—including the milk you put on cereal—count. And fluids may be contained in solids; fruits and vegetables contain water. Think about watermelon! It all adds up.

FRUIT JUICE

Actually, you don't need more than one glass of (100 percent) fruit juice a day. It's healthiest to meet requirements for fruit by eating the actual fruit, which has way more fiber than fruit juice. But here's a tip: Cutting 100 percent fruit juice with water is a refreshing way to up your fluid intake.

SPORTS DRINKS

It's best to save sports drinks for when you're exercising vigorously and/or you need to replenish your body's reserves of carbs, salts, and water because you're exercising for a very long time or when it is hot outside (see page 9).

LIMIT! DRINKS WITH ADDED SUGAR

Drinks sweetened with added sugar, like soda, "juice drinks," fruit-flavored drinks, fruit punch, fruitades, and sweetened teas, are also fluids—but these should be drunk only occasionally. Don't be lured into choosing large or supersize drinks—all for a few cents more. Who needs that amount of sugar?

The high energy content (calorie content) of these drinks isn't accompanied by many nutrients. Drinking (and eating) too many energy-dense, nutrient-poor fluids (or foods) isn't a good direction to go in.

> **F.Y.I.**
>
> The king-size soda sold at movies is 32 ounces—containing 27 teaspoons of sugar! See page 48.

THE GRAINS GROUP

CACTUS GUIDELINE: TRY TO EAT WHOLE GRAINS AT MOST MEALS. EAT A VARIETY! (GO FOR A TOTAL OF ABOUT 6–8 SERVINGS OF GRAINS A DAY.)

Each of these equals one serving:

1/2 cup of cooked oatmeal, brown rice, or whole wheat noodles/pasta (1/2 cup is about the size of a hockey puck)

1 slice of whole grain bread

1 whole grain tortilla

1 whole grain roll

1 smallish whole grain muffin

1 ounce of ready-to-eat multigrain cereal (Check the box to see what one ounce equals in "cup measurement.")

Choosing whole grains over refined grains and foods made with refined flour whenever you can is a great strategy. Scout out foods that list whole grains **first** on the ingredients list (see page 72).

When you eat brown rice instead of white rice, whole grain pasta instead of white pasta, whole grain bread instead of white bread, you will have more sustained energy.

Eating whole grain cereals will generally do better things for you in the long run than eating refined grain cereals. Regardless, avoid cereals with lots of added sugar. Who needs candy for breakfast?

SO: EASY DOES IT!

With white rice, white pasta, and white bread. And easy does it with sugary refined cereals and sugary refined baked goods like cake, cookies, doughnuts, brownies, and pastries. *Likewise: Easy does it with candy!*

A NOTE FROM THE TOOTH FAIRY

Bacteria (germs), which are always present in your mouth, are the culprits when it comes to tooth decay. These frightful little critters form sticky stuff on the surface of your teeth called *plaque*.

They hang out in the plaque and chill. When you eat something sweet, they gobble up the sugar and turn it into *acid,* which dissolves the hard enamel that coats your teeth. This can start a *cavity* (hole). (Starchy snacks can also promote tooth decay because starch breaks down into sugar once it gets into your mouth.)

Acids continue to do their dirty work for approximately twenty minutes, at which point they're neutralized (and made harmless).

If you feel a need to eat a sweet snack when you're at home, book it to the sink afterward and brush those choppers!

Good advice: If you're out and about and can't brush after eating, rinse your mouth with water.

F.Y.I.

Brush two times a day—and floss! Need a demonstration? Ask! Use toothpaste that has fluoride in it. Fluoride definitely protects your teeth from decay. If your water isn't fluoridated, please ask your dentist or health care provider if you need supplemental fluoride.

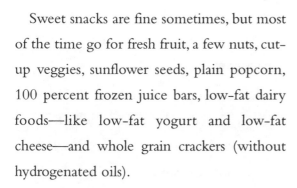

Sweet snacks are fine sometimes, but most of the time go for fresh fruit, a few nuts, cut-up veggies, sunflower seeds, plain popcorn, 100 percent frozen juice bars, low-fat dairy foods—like low-fat yogurt and low-fat cheese—and whole grain crackers (without hydrogenated oils).

F.Y.I.

Dentists recommend that kids have dental check-ups twice a year. Teeth need to be cleaned in a dentist's office routinely in order to avoid cavities and maintain the good health of your gums.

THE FRUIT GROUP
CACTUS GUIDELINE: EAT 3 SERVINGS OF FRUIT EACH DAY.

Each of these equals one serving:

1 medium whole fruit (think: size of a tennis ball)

1/4 cup dried fruit

1/2 cup of canned fruit, berries, sliced raw or cooked fruit

1/2 grapefruit

1/4 cantaloupe

11 cherries

12 grapes

7 strawberries

3/4 cup of 100 percent fruit juice (Check the label. Do you see the word "drink"? That's your tip-off. It's not what you want. Fruit juice "drinks" are often little more than flavored water with added sugar. Same with "fruit-flavored" drinks, "fruit punch," and "fruitades.")

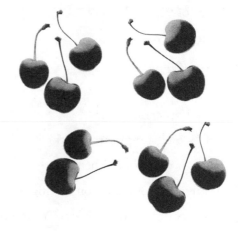

THE VEGETABLE GROUP
CACTUS GUIDELINE: EAT 4 SERVINGS OF VEGGIES
EACH DAY.

Eat lots of (colorful) vegetables—red, orange, yellow, blue, green, purple—to get the nutrients you need. White ones, too!

Red: beets, red peppers, tomatoes, red onions

Orange: carrots, yams

Yellow: squash, corn

Green: spinach, broccoli, green beans, romaine lettuce

Blue/purple: eggplant, purple cabbage

White: cabbage, cauliflower

Each of these equals one serving:

1/2 cup of cooked or sliced raw veggies

1 cup of tossed salad

3/4 cup of vegetable juice

1/3 cucumber

5 cherry tomatoes

1 medium tomato

2 cooked broccoli spears

7 to 8 (3-inch-long) carrot sticks

1/2 cup of tomato/spaghetti sauce

Tip: Why not double up on serving sizes of veggies every time you eat 'em? Your body likes lots **and lots** of veggies.

LIMIT WHITE POTATOES, ESPECIALLY FRIES!
UH?@$!#$@?!?!?

That's right!

Fast as a jackrabbit, your body converts the starch in white potatoes to sugar. And sorry, fries definitely don't have enough nutritional value to hang with the vegetable group.

Tip: Fries that are cooked in good plant oils rather than saturated fats are the better choice (see page 23).

THE PLANT OILS GROUP
CACTUS GUIDELINE: COOK WITH PLANT OILS AND USE
THEM FOR SPREADS AND DRESSINGS.

Canola, olive, soybean, corn, sunflower, peanut—your heart loves these! Use about 3 tablespoons a day, total.

EASY DOES IT—
With coconut and palm oil and oils that have been processed to be solid at room temperature (vegetable shortening and stick margarine, for example). They're not heart friendly (see page 23). Limit these.

THE NUTS AND BEANS (AND OTHER LEGUMES, INCLUDING TOFU AND OTHER SOY PROTEIN FOODS) GROUP
CACTUS GUIDELINE: EAT 1–2 SERVINGS A DAY FROM
THIS GROUP.

NUTS

Each of these equals one serving:

    2 tablespoons of peanut or almond butter

    1 ounce of nuts, which is about . . .

20 almonds or

  6 Brazil nuts or

16 cashews or

18 hazelnuts or

10 macadamia nuts or

18 pecan halves or

150 pine nuts or

45 pistachios or

14 walnut halves

> ### F.Y.I.
>
> Nuts are energy-rich and a good source of pro-tein, heart-helpin' fats, vitamins, minerals, fiber, and disease-preventing chemicals (*phytonutrients*).
>
>   Just one little ounce of nuts can turn out to be a very satisfying snack.

OH NUTS!

Unfortunately, some people are allergic to nuts. If you are, definitely don't eat them. And do check the ingredients list on food packaging (see page 72) to make sure nuts aren't hiding out in an unexpected place.

BEANS (AND LENTILS)

Each of these equals one serving:

    1/2 cup of cooked black beans, chickpeas (garbanzo beans), pinto beans, or kidney beans (think: hockey puck)

    1/2 cup of cooked lentils

TOFU AND OTHER SOY PROTEIN FOODS

Each of these equals one serving:

    about 1/2 cup of tofu or tempeh

    about a 3-ounce soyburger

THE LOW-FAT DAIRY GROUP

CACTUS GUIDELINE: EAT THREE SERVINGS EACH DAY.

Each of these equals one serving:

    1 cup of low-fat or skim milk (see page 42)

    1 cup of low-fat or non-fat yogurt

    1 1/2 to 2 ounces of low-fat or skim cheese (think: tube of lipstick)

    1/2 cup of low-fat cottage cheese

    1/2 cup of low-fat frozen yogurt or ice milk

DON'T DO DAIRY?

Calcium-fortified foods and drinks are available. So are calcium supplements, which are different from a daily (com-plete) multivitamin/multimineral supple-ment for kids. Talk to your doctor to see what he or she recommends for you. See page 15.

LIMIT:

BUTTER

Butter is a dairy product that is basically saturated fat. Yup, it's yummy spread on bread, but use it sparingly. Don't slather it!

ICE CREAM

Ice cream is too high in saturated fat to eat on a regular basis. It's a treat—an **occasional** one! Have half a cup and eat it s-l-o-w-l-y. Savor it!

Or—have you ever tried sorbet?

F.Y.I. LIGHTS, CAMERA, ACTION!

Popcorn is a nutritious, whole grain snack. But why drench each lovely puff with butter?

At the movies? Go for one of the smaller cups of popcorn, not the giant tub (even though it may only be twenty-five cents more). Ask the server to go light on the butter—or to hold the butter completely. The small (not jumbo) drink will be the perfect amount to wash it down (see page 48). Better yet—drink sparkling water!

THE LEAN ANIMAL PROTEIN GROUP

POULTRY, FISH, SEAFOOD, EGGS, LEAN RED MEAT GROUP
CACTUS GUIDELINE: EAT 1–2 SERVINGS EACH DAY.

(Remember: If you don't eat foods in this group, talk to your doc about substitutions. See page 54.)

Okay, let's break this down.

A. PLUCKY POULTRY

One serving: 2 to 3 ounces, cooked (think: deck of cards) REMOVE THE SKIN

B. DELICIOUS FISHES

One serving: 2 to 3 ounces, cooked (think: deck of cards again)

C. SCRUMPTIOUS SHELLFISH

One serving: 2 to 3 ounces, cooked (yup: deck of cards again)

D. EG-G-G-GSELLENT EGGS

One serving: 2 whole eggs or 3 egg whites (see Cholesterol, on page 24)

E. ROARIN' RED MEAT

One serving: 2 to 3 ounces, cooked (think: deck of cards)

Red meat is called red meat because it's red or dark pink when raw. It includes beef, lamb, and pork.

Most red meat has more saturated fat (see page 23) than poultry, fish, seafood, or eggs. So don't choose red meat every day. And when you do choose it, go for the leaner cuts.

F.Y.I.:
LEAN RED MEAT

Lean cuts of red meat include:

Beef: eye of round, top sirloin, extra-lean ground beef, tenderloin

Pork: tenderloin, sirloin, top loin

Lamb: leg shank

Luncheon meats: 95 to 99 percent fat free

LIMIT:

Processed, preserved, and/or cured meats like salami, bologna, hot dogs, sausages, bacon, and pepperoni aren't lean red meat—they're fatty red meat and the saturated-fattiest of all. Do minimize these.

Organ meats, such as liver, are high in cholesterol. (See page 24.)

VARY YOUR CHOICES!

Remember: Eggs, lean red meat, and certain fish should be eaten in moderation—not on a daily basis. See pages 23 (for saturated fats in meat), 24 (for eggs), and 27 (for fish).

chapter 7

FOOD: THE CELEBRATION OF LIFE

Besides giving us energy and nutrients and satisfying our appetite and providing the sensual pleasure of experiencing taste, temperature, color, and texture, food has another critical function: It brings people together.

Food links us to our culture—and to the cultures of our friends, extended families, and communities.

Preparing and serving food is a way of expressing love and affection. Eating food prepared and served to us is a way of acknowledging this loving expression.

Allow yourself to celebrate and appreciate the varied, positive experiences associated with eating: energizing your mind and body, satisfying hunger, connecting with friends and family, and celebrating yourself as a beautiful, living being nurtured by planet Earth.

SLOW FOOD

Fast food can be affordable, convenient, social—and, well, really fast. But don't forget about slow food.

Sit with your grandpa on a park bench and shell pistachio nuts.

Bring a picnic to the beach. Get sand in your sandwich. Throw a Frisbee around.

Organize a homework group on the weekend. Have nutritious snacks on hand for study breaks. Go with nuts, fruits, and vegetables with dips (see page 40 for snack suggestions).

Plan a family dinner. Expand it to include a friend.

Shopping together, fixing meals together, sitting down together at a table—and even cleaning up together after a meal are all great ways to connect with family and friends.

LEARN HOW TO COOK!

Check out a beginner's cookbook from the library. Ask the librarian to help. Librarians love to help! Find a book with simple, straightforward instructions.

Flip through it. What sounds good? Choose a recipe (or two) that fits your family's budget. If you're not allowed to use the stove, find a recipe that doesn't require cooking!

Ask your parent to schedule some time to shop and cook with you. Bring along a list of what you need (see page 112 for a Cactus Plan shopping list; make copies of it if you want).

When you cook, don't stress. Have fun! Cooking is an art form. And artists make big messes. Plan to clean up.

DO IT UP PROPER

Prettily fold the napkins.

Set the table.

Pop a daisy in a little vase.

BUT I'M SO BUSY ALL THE TIME!

Interested in doing things quickly?

Yup, sometimes that's you. Sometimes that's everybody!

—And with as little effort as possible?

Yup, sometimes that's you—and everybody else, too.

HIGHLY PROCESSED FOODS

Because we're on the run so much of the time, we often find foods in the grocery store, in restaurants, in vending machines, or in school cafeterias that have been put through complicated processes and packaged to be prepared with very little time and effort.

These foods, which include things like microwavable precooked dinners, are referred to as **highly processed** foods.

Convenient?

Oh yeah.

That's the name of the game.

Delicious?

They can be.

HOW—EVAH!

Sometimes foods are so highly processed, it's hard to distinguish what the original food source even is.

Example? Boned, precooked, breaded, re-formed frozen fish sticks . . . just pop 'em in the microwave!

But how far away from a fish is a fish stick? A fish cracker looks more like a fish!

An apple, cored and uniformly sliced by machine, sweetened with sugar and cinnamon, and baked in a crispy crust along with thousands of other little minipies, then frozen, stored in a box in a warehouse, shipped, shelved, reheated in a microwave, and sold to you in a small cardboard package isn't a bad thing. But . . .

THERE'S A TRADE-OFF

The process of turning a fish into a breaded stick and an apple into the filling of a minipie may result in the loss of nutrients and/or the gain of fats that aren't heart friendly—or both.

MINIMALLY PROCESSED FOODS

A fish stick isn't required to have fins and a tail. An apple doesn't have to have a leaf and a stem. But do let some of the food you eat be *minimally processed:* in Mama Nature's original packaging—or very close to it.

STRAIGHT UP

A crisp, ripe apple picked from a tree and washed under clear water—a straight-up apple whose shape and color and texture you can actually experience in its primal state is **very** fast food.

You can even eat it while you're walking!

Bite into it. Hear that first crunch, feel the juice run down your chin.

Mmmm.

Mmmm!

BETWEEN-MEAL SNACKS: DO!

There's an old saying: Don't eat between meals.

That's so wrong!

Snacking is an essential part of a healthy eating plan. You need these nutritional pick-me-ups.

Also, snacks keep you from getting starved and making food choices based on the fact that you're as hungry as an alligator and you want to eat anything within snapping range.

SNACK SUGGESTIONS

• Salsa with tortilla or pita chips (made **without** hydrogenated fat—check the ingredients list on the package)

• Hummus (a Middle Eastern bean dip) with whole grain crackers (made **without** hydrogenated oils—check the ingredients list on the package. And remember, "partially hydrogenated oils" do count as hydrogenated oils.)

• Whole fruits: bananas, apples, pears, pineapple slices, strawberries, grapes

• Slices of carrot, celery, green pepper, or zucchini with yogurt dips

• Whole wheat soft pretzel with mustard

- Nuts: almonds, peanuts, walnuts, mixed nuts
- Dried fruits
- Roasted soy nuts
- Tabbouleh
- Guacamole and tomato slices with pita or tortilla
- Falafel
- 100 percent frozen fruit juice bars
- Minestrone soup★
- Lentil soup★
- Chicken noodle soup★

★Read labels and try to get low-sodium soups whenever possible! Ask permission before using the stove (see page 49).

DON'T SKIP MEALS

Especially, **especially!** eat a nutritious breakfast. It's a proven scientific fact: Eating a nutritious breakfast boosts your performance in school. It enables your brain to focus and concentrate better.

GRRRRR!

Don't you know you're a worn-out, tired, grouchy, frazzled grump bucket when you don't eat?

You are!

BUT! BUT! BUT I DON'T HAVE TIME!

Yup, it's so fun to snuggle down into the covers for that extra ten minutes of sleep on school mornings! And sleep is important! (Remember: You need about eight hours of snooze time a night.)

You know your brain relies on breakfast energy to think clearly. So clearly, you need to think breakfast! It's fine to keep it simple: a bowl of whole grain cereal with 1 percent low-fat or skim milk (maybe sprinkled with a few nuts) and a piece of fruit will do the trick.

Talk to your parent about making a switch from regular orange juice to calcium-fortified orange juice and from whole milk to 1 percent low-fat or skim milk on your behalf. (Remember: Little peeps in the family may need higher-fat milk, though. Ask the pediatrician.)

GOOD BREAKFAST IDEAS

(Ask permission before using the stove. See page 49.)

- Granola or muesli (European-style granola) topped with fresh fruit, 1 percent low-fat or skim milk, or calcium-fortified soy milk
- Scrambled, poached, or hard-boiled egg with whole grain toast
- Whole grain toast with peanut or almond butter (choose nut butter without

hydrogenated oil whenever you can)

- Multigrain dry cereal, nuts with fruit juice
- Hot oatmeal with nuts, maple syrup, or honey
- Sliced banana, nutty dry whole grain cereal with 1 percent or skim milk or calcium-fortified soy milk
- Tofu, noodles with miso soup
- Whole grain bagel with low-fat cream cheese
- Multigrain pancakes/waffles with fresh fruit slices and yogurt
- Noodles with tahini sauce
- Pita with hummus
- Brown rice cakes with peanut or almond butter
- 1 percent low-fat or skim milk yogurt with raisins
- And always, some fresh fruit: apple, pear, grapes, or banana. Whatever you like!

WHY 1 PERCENT LOW-FAT OR SKIM MILK?

Since milk is **such** a great source of calcium and vitamin D, and since *whole* milk contains more saturated fat than is desirable on a day-in, day-out basis, the companies that produce milk give us options to buy milk that has most (or all) of the saturated fat removed: 1 percent low-fat or skim (fat-free) milk.

Shoot for 1 percent or skim—you'll get used to it.

F.Y.I.

A switch from whole milk to 1 percent low-fat or skim milk and other low-fat dairy products is something you can do when you're younger that can have a positive effect on your health for the rest of your life. It's so easy. Why not go for it?

WHY CALCIUM-FORTIFIED ORANGE JUICE?

Fortified means "strengthened." In this case, with calcium.

Orange juice makers add calcium to the juice before packaging to make it easy for those of us who cannot drink milk (lactose intolerant) to get the calcium we need.

Same goes for soy milk and rice milk: you can buy them fortified, too.

YOU'RE OUTTA HERE!

Spread a dollop of cold refried beans onto a tortilla, hit it with your favorite hot sauce, roll it up. Slug down a glass of orange juice or 1 percent low-fat or skim milk.

Or:

Navigate some granola into a carton of

low-fat or nonfat yogurt—stir it up and you're good to go. A slice of cold pizza? Lift the lid and sneak it out of the box.

An inviting carton of rice, pea pods, and chicken left over from last night? Snag it before somebody else does!

Wash it down with 1 percent low-fat or skim milk, orange juice, or water.

Pop a slice of whole grain toast into the toaster. While it's toasting, hunt down that elusive jar of peanut butter in the back of the fridge. Knock back a glass of fruit juice or low-fat milk. Allergic to nuts? Then slather some low-fat cream cheese on the toast instead. Fold it in half and you're out the door.

WAIT WAIT WAIT!

If your doctor recommends it, don't forget your one daily (complete) multivitamin/multimineral supplement for kids.

F.Y.I.

If you eat too fast, your hunger mechanism won't get the message that you're full! Chew, taste, enjoy your food. That way you won't overeat!

HOW MUCH ENERGY DO YOU NEED?

How much energy do you need in a day?

It depends on what stage of puberty you're in (how fast you're growing) and how physically active you are.

Think in terms of eating three nutritious meals each day and a couple of healthy snacks in between.

That should do it.

F.Y.I.

During puberty, kids often gain weight and then grow taller—relatively quickly.

It's important to understand that an appropriate plan for many overweight adolescents is to maintain your current weight. Follow a nutritious eating and healthy physical activity plan (like The Cactus Plan).

In time, you'll grow taller. Your weight will then "fit" your height. Check your individual situation out with your doctor.

Also, crash/fad "diets" promote unhealthy eating practices and attitudes. And guess what. They don't work! Frequent "dieting" by teen girls is related to *binge eating* (overeating), which results in weight gain over time.

WEIGHT CONCERNS?

It takes a health care professional to determine if you're in a healthy weight range for whatever stage of puberty you're in.

If you have weight concerns, make an appointment to discuss them with your doctor. Ask to see a registered dietitian.

Your doctor needs to be involved in evaluating your growth and determining whether you should gain weight, maintain your weight, slow your weight gain, or lose weight while you're going through puberty.

HOW THE ENERGY INTAKE/ENERGY OUTPUT BALANCE RELATES TO WEIGHT

Over time, if you take in about the same amount of energy as you use up through growth, metabolism, and physical activity, your weight will remain in a healthy range.

Back in the day, humans could bank on going through some pretty harsh times, living off the land. At times, food was scarce.

People who were genetically programmed to use energy efficiently were able to survive on less food, stay healthier, live longer, reproduce more—and pass their survival gene (called the *thrifty gene*) on to their kids.

WE'RE DESIGNED TO KEEP ENERGY IN RESERVE—

—In the event of getting lost in the wilderness, marooned on a desert island, or having food sources dwindle.

This isn't likely to happen at this place and time.

FOOD IS NOW EVERYWHERE

Plentiful, fast, convenient, and always within your reach. Think about malls, highways, movie theaters, and amusement parks. You smell and see food everywhere, tempting you to eat even though you are not hungry.

WAYS TO AVOID EXCESS ENERGY (CALORIE) INTAKE

1. Manage your hunger by eating regular, balanced meals and snacks. S-L-O-W-L-Y. Enjoy them!

2. Pay attention to portion size. Moderation is key.

3. Eat lots and lots of fruits and vegetables.

4. Drink plenty of water. Limit sweetened beverages. Don't supersize soft drinks (sodas).

5. Follow nutritional guidelines (see page 30) when it comes to eating foods that are very high in added sugar, saturated fat, and/or *trans* fat. Occasional means: sparingly. Every once in a while. Not often.

6. Pay attention to—and follow—your hunger cues. Eat when you're hungry—and stop when you're full.

7. Please also pay attention to the effects that advertising may be having on you. There's a difference between being hungry and having an urge to eat (see page 98).

HEADS UP!

Do you have a friend who seems totally stressed about eating or not eating? Are you? If so, tell your parent, teacher, or another trusted adult.

Sometimes, emotional problems take the form of extremely negative behaviors related to food and physical activity.

These kinds of problems always require help from a mental health care professional (see page 106).

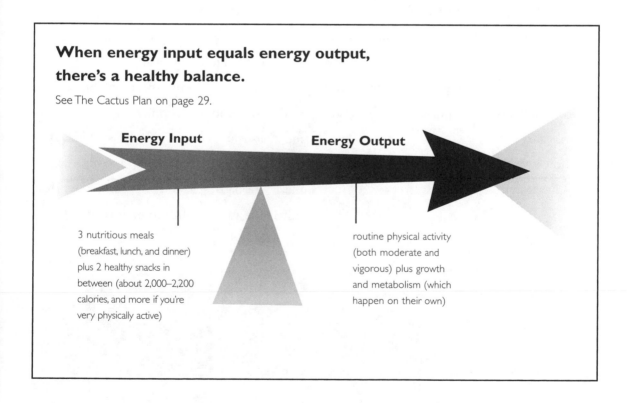

When energy input equals energy output, there's a healthy balance.

See The Cactus Plan on page 29.

Energy Input

Energy Output

3 nutritious meals (breakfast, lunch, and dinner) plus 2 healthy snacks in between (about 2,000–2,200 calories, and more if you're very physically active)

routine physical activity (both moderate and vigorous) plus growth and metabolism (which happen on their own)

chapter 8

TAKING CHARGE

FOOD CHOICES

Smell the intoxicating scent of a warm, squishy cinnamon bun as you walk through the mall? Hey! You! It's callin' your name!

Food choices are influenced by such a wide range of things—from TV commercials to friends and family to neighborhood stores and local restaurants to vending machines and school cafeterias.

Choices are also influenced by the media and advertising.

WANT TO EAT HEALTHIER? DO!

If your friends don't, so what. Don't hound them.

And don't compare the nutritional value of what they're eating to what you're eating. Nobody likes to be compared.

Also: It's mighty unclassy and highly uncool to dish on food that another individual is eating that you personally find distasteful. And that includes meat if you're a vegetarian or meat alternatives if you're a carnivore! Treat others the way you like to be treated.

How many ads do you see on TV for vegetables, whole fruits, whole grain products, fish, seafood, nuts, and beans?

Hmmm. Not many!

Fast-food marketers want your $$$! Be aware of how TV commercials influence your food choices—so you can make healthy ones. See page 98.

NUTRITIONAL BOOSTING

So many meals and snacks can be given a quick, extra nutritional boost without much effort on your part.

ORDERING PIZZA?

Onions, mushrooms, black olives, sliced tomatoes, green peppers—even pineapple—can be added. Or go for the veggie combo!

STOPPING BY THE DELI?

There are many ways to up the nutritional content of deli sandwiches. Here are two:

1. Ask for whole grain bread
2. Say yes to sliced tomatoes and lettuce

You can also:

• Ask for mayonnaise to be spread lightly or try subbing mustard for mayo. Choose lean meats like sliced turkey or chicken. Want red meat? Stick with lean roast beef rather than bologna or salami.

• If they're available, ask to sample partially skim milk cheeses to see which ones you like. Add a slice to your sandwich.

FAST-FOOD RESTAURANT?

Fast-food restaurants are part of our culture. Meet with your buds. Talk and laugh. But why order the same old, same old?

Chicken can be a welcome change of pace from burgers. Chicken fajita pita (fa-heeta pee-ta)? Yes! Grilled-chicken sandwich? Go for it.

Fast food can also include California rolls (sushi), rice bowls topped with veggies, and other quick meals from our wide range of cultures. Experiment!

BE THE BUNNY

Add a green salad to your order.

Dressings made with plant oils are just so good for you! They're energy rich. A smallish glug or blob should do the trick.

Experiment with light dressings, like raspberry vinaigrette. It's fine to ask for dressing on the side so you can taste it—and be in charge of how much you use.

SHARE

Sure, we could eat a million fries—but why? They're so superloaded with energy (calories), we don't need a whole bagful. Share an order. Construct a little ketchup-dipping station and sidle up with a friend.

Milk shake? Ask for an extra cup and split it.

Deep-fried chicken strips or nuggets? A few will do. Let others poach. Pass them around.

YEE-HAW!

Americans are famous for our Texas-size portions (big). But listen up, pardner:

SUPERSIZING

Godzilla-size soft drinks, jumbo fries, and burgers stacked one on top of another, topped with cheese and bacon, are fast-food meals that provide a level of energy you just don't require on an everyday basis.

Ads on TV make it seem like we can and should eat these day in, day out for our whole lives and not suffer harmful results or consequences, but that's not true.

If you hit up fast food often, self-regulate on portion size.

Like burgers? Have a regular burger, a regular order of fries, and a **small** soft drink. Still thirsty?

Drink water.

AT HOME?

Keep a stash of cold, crisp, colorful cut-up veggies in a plastic bag in the fridge: celery, carrots, red, green, yellow peppers, sliced summer squash, sliced zucchini—whatever. Maybe your parent could be recruited to help you slice 'em up.

You may have to guard the refrigerator, though—because once they're sliced, iced, and there for the taking, you can expect some sneak attacks on the storehouse from family members.

> Make sure you have permission before using sharp knives, and if you don't feel comfortable using them, ask for help.
>
> Finished slicing? Don't drop that knife in a sinkful of soapy water. Someone might get cut when they reach in. Carefully clean the knife and put it back where it belongs.

CHIP TIP

Chips vary in nutritional value. Many are made from whole grains (corn, for example) and baked or fried in plant oil (rather than in saturated or hydrogenated oil). Nab those.

Dip 'em in salsa: canned, jarred, or homemade.

COLD OUT?

Warm up.

Va-room! Soup up a can of soup (low sodium if you have it) by adding extra goodies: carrots, peas, corn, beans, broccoli, tomatoes, and other nutritional heavy hitters.

GET PERMISSION BEFORE USING THE STOVE

Not confident? Ask for help from an adult.

SAFETY TIPS

Keep curtains, dishcloths, oven mitts, paper towels, and other flammable things away from the burner. Tie back your hair if it's long. Filmy, billowy, loose clothes aren't safe for chefs of any age.

Make sure the pot handle isn't sticking out where you could accidentally topple it.

Don't allow the phone or TV to distract you. Don't leave the room when the stove is on.

Steam burns! Use a pot holder or oven mitt to lift the lid from a pot full of hot food. Lift the lid in the direction that's **away from you,** away from your face.

HOT OUT?

Chill with a chilly snack.

Freeze your favorite juice in an ice tray. While you're at it, slice a couple of bananas in half (the long way), carefully seal them in a sealable plastic bag (squeeze the air out first), and pop 'em in the freezer.

Forget they're there. You've got other things to do than wait for fruit to freeze.

A few hours later, when you're really hungry, grouchy, and hot . . . Yay! You'll remember them! Have an icy banana and add the frozen juice cubes to a glass of bubbly water (seltzer).

ON THE ROAD AGAIN?

Travel with a couple of apples, a plastic bottle of water, and some nibblies: a small bag of granola, an energy bar, some dried fruit, and/or nuts in your pack or purse. Sound like rabbit food? What's not to like about a rabbit?

AT SCHOOL?

Why not turn your locker (or pack) into a minimart? Apples and oranges last quite a while. Energy bars also have a good shelf life—when sealed up in their original wrappers. (But check the ingredients list—some energy bars are the nutritional equivalents of candy bars!)

Mixed nuts are a good standby. So are individually wrapped packets of whole grain crackers or chips. Bottled waters (plastic, and recycle, please) can hold their own over a reasonable period of time.

> The ants come marching one by one, hurrah. And some schools even have—yikes!—a roach problem. Keep your snacks sealed in containers or closed up in sealable plastic bags.

Snacks can't last forever in the depths of a backpack or rubble of a locker. Check the expiration date of provisions that have been around for a while.

> How do you choose an energy bar? Look at the ingredients list.
>
> • Choose bars that contain whole grains (like oats, millet, and barley).
>
> • Go for bars that don't contain hydrogenated or partially hydrogenated oils.
>
> • Nuts, nut butter, or dried fruits are great additions (if you're not allergic to nuts).
>
> • Sugar should be listed toward the **end** of the ingredients list (see page 72). Sugar has many names, including: glucose, galactose, dextrose, fructose, sucrose, lactose, maltose, corn syrup, brown sugar, and corn sweetener. Sugar is sugar—none is more healthy than another.

FOOD CHOICES AT SCHOOL

What's available to eat in your school cafeteria—and on your school site?

IS SOME IMPROVEMENT CALLED FOR?

Get some friends, maybe a parent or two, and a couple of teachers together and ask for a meeting with your principal to discuss how your school can increase nutritional awareness and expand and improve food choices for students. Keep the tone of the meeting upbeat and positive. Don't make accusations that put anyone on the spot.

Could you conduct a faculty/student survey for input and ideas?

Some possible topics to put on the table:

Is 1 percent low-fat or skim milk available in the cafeteria? How about calcium-fortified orange juice? It's such a delicious alternative to milk.

How about getting more colorful fruits and vegetables on the menu? What about a salad bar? Veggie burgers?

Could à la carte fruit (sold separately) be made available at lunch? (Locally grown? All the better.)

Can the vending machines and snack bars be stocked with more tasty and healthy varieties? Maybe your parent-teacher association could get involved.

OFFENDING VENDING

Soda and candy calling to you from strategically placed machines around your school campus?

If these machines are going to be in your face five days a week throughout your growth spurt, ask for equal time for foods that do really good things for you—including boosting your academic and athletic performance.

Ask that 1 percent low-fat or skim milk, 100 percent fruit juice, cold water, whole grain chips and whole grain crackers, nuts, dried fruits, and other healthy snacks be included as choices in your school's vending machines.

NEED SUPPORT?

So many people care! Look for support among faculty (including the school nurse), student council reps, parents, and other students. Suggest that your school form a committee that focuses on nutrition and safe, fun physical activities (both competitive and noncompetitive) during and after school. Think of it: everything from Ping-Pong to salsa dancing could be considered.

Name for the committee? How about Advisory Committee on Healthy Eating and Active Living? That sounds official!

AND WHY NOT GO FOR THE GOLD: A GARDEN!

Food gardens are springing up in schools all over the United States, including in the middle of cities.

Developing and using food gardens as teaching tools is really catching on.

How much fun would it be for you and your friends at school to get some exercise, fresh air, and bonding time while you dig in the dirt, plant and harvest your own crops, and maybe grow beautiful flowers?

While you're learning interesting information about science—are there other subjects that tie in?

The same sun rises and sets over the city as it does over the country. Plants need soil, water, and sunshine.

Got those three things in your schoolyard?

Yup, you do!

Too much asphalt and concrete?

Aboveground gardens in great big wooden boxes work. Parents can help you build 'em.

Why not set up a meeting with a teacher and/or principal to discuss the possibilities?

Make it happen.

chapter **9**

BEING VEGETARIAN

Considering becoming a vegetarian?

Why not share this book—and this chapter in particular—with your parent so you can discuss the pros and cons?

INTRO: VEGETARIAN FOOD PLANS

There are lots of ways of being a vegetarian.

Generally speaking, being a vegetarian means that you don't eat red meat, fish, seafood, pork, or poultry.

Many vegetarians do eat eggs and/or dairy products.

"Modified" vegetarians also include fish and seafood in their plan.

VEGANS—PLANTS TO THE MAX

Vegans are vegetarians who don't eat **any** food that comes from an animal. Zero, none.

Vegans don't eat red meat, fish, seafood, poultry, pork, eggs, dairy products—or

honey, since honey is technically an animal product. (Some also avoid leather, wool, cashmere, beeswax, and all products that come from animals.)

WHY BE A VEGETARIAN?

The reasons why people choose to be vegetarian vary.

Some make the choice for cultural, religious, or philosophical reasons. Some do it because they feel it's the healthiest eating plan—for them.

UM, HOW CAN WE SAY THIS?

Becoming a vegetarian during adolescence calls for a serious commitment. If you're up to the challenge, go for it.

If you're not, wait until you are.

Regardless of the motivation (or inspiration), being a vegetarian or a vegan works for adolescents **only** if you meet your nutritional needs for growth, metabolism, and physical activity.

MEETING YOUR NEEDS

If you want to exclude all animal foods, like red meat, poultry, pork, eggs, fish and other seafood, and/or dairy, you'll need to find substitutions for these foods because they are such excellent sources of nutrients—including calcium, iron, zinc, B vitamins, and *complete protein* (containing all of the essential **amino acids** that our bodies need).

Before eliminating animal sources of protein from your eating plan, you need to be completely sure of how to make the correct replacements.

WELL PLANNED

A well-planned vegetarian eating pattern works for teens—but "well" and "planned" are the key words here.

Maybe your family, cultural, and religious traditions set you on a healthy vegetarian path years and years ago. If so, you will undoubtedly have a healthy eating pattern in place.

But if a vegetarian eating pattern is new to you, work with a registered dietitian or other health care professional who can guide you as you establish a pattern that conforms with healthy vegetarian principles and practices.

FAMILY AND PEER PRESSURE

It's understandable that teens who become vegetarians face a certain amount of resistance from parents, grandparents, and peers.

Teens are often on the run. A poorly planned vegan eating pattern can set you up for nutritional deficiencies.

Quantity and quality of nutrients are the issues—and nutrients must be present in a form that is readily usable so that the body can absorb them effectively.

However, there's no reason why you can't win the support of your family and friends— by becoming fully aware of the responsibilities that go along with adopting a vegetarian eating plan and making (and keeping) a serious commitment to achieving a healthy eating routine.

KEY CONCERNS FOR ADOLESCENT VEGETARIANS
1. PROTEIN

Protein is basically about growth and cell repair.

A vegetarian plan that includes eggs and dairy products covers the protein requirement with no problem.

Good plant sources of protein for vegans include whole wheat bread, brown rice, almonds, peas, pumpkin seeds, chickpeas (garbanzo beans), peanut butter, quinoa, tofu, soy milk, and lentils. But be aware that covering all of our protein needs requires that certain foods be eaten in combination: rice and beans, for example.

2. ENERGY INTAKE

All is good with a vegetarian plan, provided your nutritional requirements are met—and you get enough energy to support growth.

An adolescent girl needs energy (calories) from a wide variety of sources rich in a variety of nutrients: three nutritious meals and a couple of healthy snacks.

Carbohydrates found in whole grain foods, fruits, nuts, and legumes will keep your energy level right up there. So eat these throughout the day.

Most leafy vegetables aren't energy dense (calorie rich), but lots of plant-based foods are. Beans, starchy vegetables, avocados, and nuts are examples of energy-dense vegan foods.

3. VITAMIN D

Vitamin D just isn't found in plant foods at all. Ten to fifteen minutes of sunshine on the hands and face, a daily (complete) multivitamin/multimineral supplement for kids (if recommended by a doctor), and fortified/enriched foods like soy milk can bring vegans right up to speed in the vitamin D department.

4. CALCIUM

If you drink 1 percent low-fat or skim milk and eat dairy products, you'll cover your calcium requirement.

Vegan diets should include a variety of calcium-fortified foods like orange juice, soy milk, and tofu.

Other good sources of calcium for vegans are okra, sesame seeds, collard and turnip greens, soybeans, figs, tempeh, almond butter, broccoli, bok choy, commercial soy yogurt, calcium-enriched breakfast cereals, and breads fortified with calcium.

Daily (complete) multivitamin/multimineral supplements for kids only partly fulfill the calcium requirement. Vegan calcium supplements are available; check with your doctor.

SUPERSLEUTH

Oxalic acid found in spinach, chard, and beet greens reduces calcium absorption. These plant foods are absolutely great for you—but when considering dietary plant sources for calcium, include **other** dark green vegetables like broccoli or bok choy.

5. IRON

Plant foods that are good sources of iron include raisins, dried fruit, soybeans, lentils, black-eyed peas, blackstrap molasses, firm tofu, chickpeas (garbanzo beans), kidney beans, and pinto beans. Iron-fortified cereals and iron-fortified whole grain breads are also very good.

Daily (complete) multivitamin/multimineral supplements for kids contain iron. Should you take one each day? Ask your doc.

6. VITAMIN B-12

Essential for healthy blood and healthy nerves, vitamin B-12 is found in animal foods, not plant foods. Please take special note of this.

Vegetarians eating no animal products need to consult with a doctor about taking a daily (complete) multivitamin/ multimineral supplement for kids and/or eating the right fortified foods to get the B-12 they need.

Vitamin B-12 deficiency (not enough of the vitamin over time) can cause severe anemia (see page 18) and irreversible damage to the nervous system. Symptoms don't appear right away because the body stores and recycles this vitamin for a while.

However, vitamin B-12 is plentiful in fortified foods: breakfast cereals (Grape-Nuts is a good one), fortified soy milk, B-12-fortified meat "stand-in" products, and vegetarian-

support-formula nutritional yeast (for example, Red Star nutritional yeast).

Supersleuth: Look for cyanocobalamin on the ingredients list. That's the form of vitamin B-12 that's best absorbed.

> ## HEADS UP!
> Tempeh, miso, and seaweed are often labeled as having lots of B-12, but the B-12 may have been changed by the processing. Don't rely on these.

7. ZINC

Essential for growth, development, and a wide range of the body's functions, zinc can be found in wheat germ, legumes, beans, nuts, tofu, seeds—and daily (complete) multivitamin/multimineral supplements for kids.

VEGETARIAN VARIETY

Mmmm-mmm! How's this for variety? Stir-fried veggies, fortified breakfast cereals, seeds, multigrain toast, orange juice, frozen fruit desserts, three-bean salad, dates, apples, macaroni, fruit smoothies, popcorn, spaghetti, vegetarian baked beans, vegetarian refried beans, pumpkin seeds, tortillas, tofu lasagna, guacamole, meatless chili, hummus, corn chowder, muffins with fruit spread, pasta salad, sandwiches with white bean pâté with lemon and garlic, vegetable soup, rice pudding, fava beans, banana muffins, sunflower seeds, spinach pie, eggless French toast and pancakes made with soy milk, collards, black beans with marinated tomatoes, bean burritos, flavored brown rice, meatless spaghetti sauce, sesame tahini, grilled marinated vegetables, grape leaves, cantaloupe, eggplant spreads, mustard greens, turnip greens, bok choy, textured vegetable protein, blackstrap molasses, apple juice, V8 juice, margarine, falafel, corn fritters, soy hot dogs, veggie burgers . . .

SAMPLE VEGAN DINNER

(Get permission before using the stove, and if you need help from your parent, do ask for it.) Brown rice, maybe seasoned with herbs and lemon and sprinkled with chopped nuts or sunflower seeds, salad, beans, and fruit.

Brown rice takes about forty minutes to cook, so plan ahead. Follow the directions on the package.

While the rice is cooking, make a crisp, colorful salad with tomatoes, radishes, green onions, carrots, peppers, avocados, and a couple of different kinds of leafy green lettuce—topped with kidney beans, chickpeas (garbanzo beans), and sunflower seeds.

Dressing? How about olive oil and vinegar, a little salt and pepper? That's simple. (Use one

tablespoon of vinegar for every three tablespoons of olive oil.)

> ### EASY VINAIGRETTE DRESSING
>
> I tablespoon of vinegar (white wine, balsamic) for every 3 tablespoons of extra-virgin olive oil
>
> I teaspoon of French mustard (optional)
>
> Put the vinegar, olive oil, and French mustard in a small jar with a cover. Cover tightly and shake until all ingredients are combined. Season with salt or soy sauce and pepper.

Vegetarian refried beans conveniently come in a can. Just heat 'em up when the rice is almost done. Put the rice and beans right next to each other on a plate. Pile on some salad or cooked vegetables. Pretty!

Munch an apple or scarf an orange for dessert.

(We'll be **right** over!)

Want more information and ideas about a vegetarian eating plan?

Check out:

The Vegetarian Resource Group

http://www.vrg.org

Produce Marketing Association and Produce for Better Health Foundation

http://www.aboutproduce.com

chapter 10

GERM BUSTERS

BARF-O-RAMA?

No thanks.

Leaving food out of the fridge for too long, undercooking food, nuking food unevenly, cooking or reheating food at too low a temperature, thawing/marinating food on the counter instead of in the fridge, keeping leftovers too long in the fridge, cooling large quantities of food the wrong way, having the wrong refrigerator/freezer temperature setting, overstuffing the fridge so it doesn't work right, eating from unclean plates and utensils, and preparing food on unclean countertops or with unclean hands are all common causes of food-borne illness. So listen up!

FOOD-BORNE ILLNESSES: WE DON'T WANT 'EM

Bacteria and viruses are way too small to see, and they're everywhere. Most bacteria are harmless to humans. Some of them are actually helpful to humans.

But some of them are up to no good, and those are the ones we're talking about here: the weasels responsible for food-borne illnesses (illnesses you get from food).

Food-borne illnesses are caused by our bodies becoming invaded by certain germs—bacteria and viruses—or by little critters called **parasites.** Illnesses may also be caused by toxins (poisons) produced by bacteria contained in food.

Parasites take up residence in our digestive systems and/or other organs and happily live there until we can drive them out with medications. We avoid getting them in the first place by killing them through heat or by washing them off what we're about to eat—before we eat it.

GERMS

Happily, we do have our own built-in germ patrol (the immune system). Our immune system is set up to zap bacteria, viruses, and other teeny invaders that get into our bloodstream or infect the lining of our gastrointestinal tract.

When disease-causing bacteria and viruses come on too strong, they make us sick until our immune systems can beat them back and/or kill them off completely.

SYMPTOMS

Sometimes people with food-borne illness think they have the flu, but they don't. They're sick, sick, sick from some lousy food or drink they inadvertently consumed.

One famous and very unpleasant symptom of certain food-borne illnesses is the Green Apple Two-step, better known as diarrhea.

Other symptoms may include vomiting, headache, fever, cramping, and utter exhaustion. But symptoms vary. And they can occur within a half hour of eating contaminated food or they can show up days, or even weeks, later.

Food-borne illness can especially be a problem to pregnant women, infants, old people, and people whose bodies can't fight infection very well.

LIQUIDS NEED TO BE DRUNK . . .

. . . to replace fluids lost through vomiting and/or diarrhea. When symptoms are severe (bloody diarrhea, excessive nausea and vomiting, high fever), food-borne illness can become a medical emergency. Get medical help, pronto.

In some cases, a medical professional will need to figure out what kind of germs or critters are involved and exactly what medication to use to get rid of 'em. So preserve the evidence. If the suspect food is still available, wrap it, mark it DANGER, and freeze it. Save all packaging materials. You may be asked to make these things available for testing and/or alerting the public.

Also: If the food was served at a large gathering, a restaurant, or a food-service facility, or if it is a commercial product, call your local public health department.

ESPECIALLY WATCH OUT FOR THE LITTLE PEEPS

If a baby in your care develops vomiting or diarrhea, notify a responsible adult and call the pediatrician! Dehydration (loss of fluids) in infants can become a life-threatening medical emergency.

HOW DO GERMS GET ONTO THE FOOD IN THE FIRST PLACE?

1. THE FOOD IS PREPARED IN AN UNCLEAN MANNER AND GERMS FROM THE ENVIRONMENT OR FROM THE COOK'S HANDS GET ONTO IT.

PREVENTION

Pay close attention to where raw meat, poultry, and fish and other seafood are transported or stored—so the packages won't drip juices on other stuff.

Wash your hands with soap and water after using the bathroom, changing a diaper, or playing with your pets. Count to thirty—slowly—as you wash. Rinse well.

Have a cut or sore on your hand? If you can't cover it effectively, don't prepare food for others. (You need plastic gloves to be effective, since cloth gets wet and becomes unprotective.)

Wash your hands (as above) before preparing and serving food. Prepare and serve food on clean surfaces and with clean kitchen utensils. Germs have a field day on sponges and dishcloths; end the jamboree by replacing sponges often and washing dishcloths in hot soapy water in the washing machine.

Opening a can? First, rinse off the top in running water to keep dirt from getting into the food.

Wash your hands very well (as above) after handling raw meat, poultry, fish or other seafood, or eggs. Also: Don't let germs from raw food get onto ready-to-eat food by way of contaminated utensils, dishes, pans, or countertops. Wash anything that comes in contact with raw meat, poultry, fish or other seafood, or eggs with hot soapy water—immediately. Some households have separate cutting boards for meats and fruits/veggies.

2. GERMS AND/OR PARASITES ARE IN THE FOOD RIGHT FROM THE GET-GO.

Raw meat, poultry, fish or other seafood, and eggs aren't sterile (germ-free) or parasite-free when we buy them from the store. We have to make them germ- and parasite-free by cooking them at a high enough temperature to kill the little beasts.

Germs also love to lurk in unpasteurized (un-heat-treated) dairy products, untreated juices—and raw bean and alfalfa sprouts!

Fruits and vegetables aren't completely clean, either.

PREVENTION

CAREFULLY WASH FRESH FRUITS AND FRESH VEGETABLES UNDER RUNNING WATER BEFORE EATING THEM.

When appropriate, you can use a little veggie brush to get dirt out of the crevices!

DRINK AND EAT JUICE AND DAIRY PRODUCTS, INCLUDING MILK, CHEESE, AND YOGURT, THAT ARE PASTEURIZED (HEAT TREATED).

COOK MEAT, POULTRY, FISH, AND EGGS AT A HIGH ENOUGH TEMPERATURE. COOK EGGS UNTIL YOLK AND WHITE ARE FIRM.

If you don't already own a food thermometer (different from the kind of thermometer people use to check for a fever!), put one on the family's shopping list.

FOLLOW MICROWAVING TEMPERATURE INSTRUCTIONS ON THE PACKAGE; COVER, TURN, AND STIR IF NECESSARY SO FOOD COOKS EVENLY. (DON'T PUT METAL—INCLUDING FOIL—IN THE MICROWAVE.)

3. GERMS ARE THERE BECAUSE THE FOOD IS ALREADY SPOILED.

Check expiration dates before you buy and/or eat packaged food. And be aware that certain foods deteriorate even if they've been refrigerated and packaged properly.

COOK FOODS TO A SAFE TEMPERATURE

Recommended Safe Cooking Temperatures

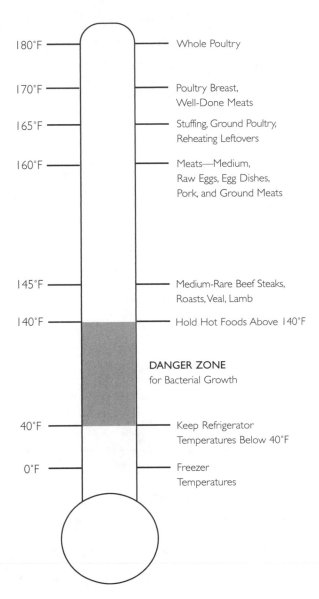

180°F — Whole Poultry

170°F — Poultry Breast, Well-Done Meats

165°F — Stuffing, Ground Poultry, Reheating Leftovers

160°F — Meats—Medium, Raw Eggs, Egg Dishes, Pork, and Ground Meats

145°F — Medium-Rare Beef Steaks, Roasts, Veal, Lamb

140°F — Hold Hot Foods Above 140°F

DANGER ZONE
for Bacterial Growth

40°F — Keep Refrigerator Temperatures Below 40°F

0°F — Freezer Temperatures

These food temperatures are for home use. They are not intended for processing, institutional, or food-service preparation.

Adapted from: US Department of Agriculture Dietary Guidelines for Americans 2000.

PREVENTION

Green mystery fuzz? Liquid lettuce? Yup. We've all seen it. The outer limit for keeping leftovers in the fridge is three days. Some things need to be eaten up—or thrown out—sooner. If in doubt, throw it out. Smelling won't give you any answers, since some spoiled food smells fine.

Nononono! Don't "taste test" food that you think might be a goner. What if you're right?

Some bacteria produce bad chemicals that are not destroyed by cooking, even though the bacteria will be. So cooking at a high temperature isn't going to solve the problem. Food that is spoiled should be tha-rown out!

4. GERMS ARE THERE BECAUSE THE FOOD HAS LINGERED TOO LONG IN THE DANGER ZONE!

Yup—there's a temperature range that disease-causing bacteria just love. To prove it, they multiply, multiply, and multiply more. The danger zone is from forty degrees to 140 degrees Fahrenheit (F).

Foods left in the danger zone for more than two hours, or one hour in temperatures over ninety degrees, may make people really sick. Picnickers and barbecuers, beware! Use those icy coolers!

PREVENTION

When keeping cooked food hot, the food needs to be continuously kept at a temperature above 140 degrees F.

Leftover foods (or foods that have been cooked and cooled) should be reheated to at least 165 degrees F. (Hot!) And: When reheating food in the oven, crank the oven temperature up to at least 325 degrees until the food reaches an internal temp of 165 degrees F.

Cold food needs to be kept chilled—below forty degrees F. (Cold!) Your fridge should be set at thirty-nine degrees F or below.

Within two hours, or within one hour if the outside (or inside) temperature is ninety degrees F or above, put leftovers in the fridge, in the freezer, or in a cooler well stocked with ice or commercial freezing gels.

Divide large amounts of leftovers into small, shallow containers for quick cooling in the fridge. Maximum depth (and thickness): two inches. Slice meats and refrigerate; don't just shove the whole roast (or turkey) in.

Don't partially cook food with the plan of finishing the job later. This increases the risk of bacteria growing in it.

Check out package and jar labels to see how food is supposed to be stored. (Mayo, hot sauce, and ketchup, once opened, need to be kept in the fridge.)

Transfer canned foods into plastic containers for storage in the fridge.

Don't stuff that refrigerator! Air needs to circulate for the system to work right.

Marinate and thaw food in the fridge, not on the counter. Or thaw it in the microwave, using the defrost setting—then cook it right away.

You can also defrost frozen food in cold running water or submerged in cold water with cold water running over it fast enough to break up and float off loose particles in an overflow.

EEEW!

After all this germ talk, you may have decided you've suddenly lost your appetite forever. However, if you want more info, call the Food and Drug Administration's food information line at 1-888-723-3366.

Specialists are available from 10 A.M. to 4 P.M. (Eastern Standard Time) Monday through Friday.

Recorded info: 24/7.

Or visit Food Safety: Kids, Teens & Educators at http://www.foodsafety.gov/~fsg/fsgkids.html.

LAST BUT NOT LEAST

Please wash your hands before you eat.

chapter 11

A PROPER SHOPPER

It's really important to have healthy food and drinks available in your home. When you're hungry or thirsty, you'll reach for those.

Some families keep a running list of things they're out of—or running low on. Why not post one on your fridge or on a cupboard?

Before putting that milk carton back in the fridge with just a splash left in the bottom, be a hero: Add 1 percent low-fat or skim milk to the list. Nobody will be stuck having to put orange juice on cereal in the morning!

SHOPPING GUIDELINES

Do you have shopping and/or food preparation responsibilities for yourself and/or others?

You can use The Cactus Plan shopping list on page 112 to help guide your choices.

Check it out. (Fine to copy it.)

READY TO GO?

Whether it's your list or ours, do take a few minutes to make out some kind of shopping list before you go to the store. Then you'll get what you actually need.

Tank up on a glass of water and have a nutritious snack. That way you won't be starving and dying of thirst and tempted to snag icy soft drinks or buy sugary treats or other snacks that are expensive and low in nutritional value.

FOOD SAFETY SHOPPING TIPS

Perishable refers to food that spoils relatively quickly at room temperature. So it's kept refrigerated or frozen in the store—like dairy products and chicken.

When you shop, pick out perishable foods last. That way, they'll stay cooler longer, since they'll be chillin' in the refrigerator cases while you shop for the other things you need.

After shopping, you'll need to get the perishable stuff into your fridge, pronto. Plan your day accordingly.

BUYING CANNED FOODS?

Check each can to make sure that it isn't dented. Or bulging! A bulging can is evidence that the food inside has spoiled and bacteria are producing some kind of stinko gas. (Likewise, if you open a can with a can opener and it hisses at you—uh, don't even think about eating what's inside. Throw the whole can out!)

Is the can sticky? Good grief—don't buy it. It may be leaking.

To help others, please point it out to a store employee.

BUYING FOOD IN JARS?

Check to make sure the jar isn't cracked and that the lid isn't bulging or loose. Jars need to remain well sealed for food to stay fresh.

BUY EGGS THAT ARE REFRIGERATED

Open the box first and check to make sure the eggs aren't cracked or broken.

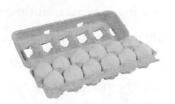

BUYING DAIRY?

Check the "use by" or "sell by" date on cartons of milk, cream, cottage cheese, cream cheese, yogurt, sour cream, etc. Pick the ones that will stay freshest the longest and don't buy any whose expiration dates have passed or will pass before you'll use them up.

Remember: Buy only pasteurized dairy products. (Check the label.)

BUYING FROZEN POULTRY, FISH, SEAFOOD, OR LEAN MEAT?

Take only packages that are below the freezer's "frost line" (not the ones sitting on top). If you can see into the package, check for signs of ice or frost, because this could mean that the contents have thawed and refrozen. Don't buy packages that are open, torn, or crushed.

PUT RAW MEAT, POULTRY, FISH, AND SEAFOOD IN SEPARATE PLASTIC BAGS

Find a place in your cart where juices from the meat, fish, and poultry packages can't drip on your other food.

OKAY. LET'S HIT IT.

Fruits and vegetables. What's in season?

Head to the fresh produce section and get ready to pinch.

Be aware that some fruits continue to ripen after being picked; plums, peaches, and apricots are examples. Others don't continue to ripen once plucked from the plant; strawberries and oranges are examples.

Frozen and canned vegetables are convenient and nutritionally sound alternatives to fresh produce. Canned beans are a fast way to up the beans and legumes in your daily plan. Ask your family to stock them. When buying canned fruit, look for those with natural juices, not syrup.

Load up your cart.

LOCALLY GROWN

Buying locally grown fruits and vegetables supports local farmers; this is great. They're also dependably fresh and delicious—although sometimes a little more expensive than produce grown on a grander scale.

Lots of people think it's worth a little extra money to buy locally grown fruits and vegetables.

Have a weekly farmers' market in your area? Take a field trip there with your family and/or friends.

Enjoy some quality time together, out in the fresh air, as you pick up a few days' worth of fresh, crisp fruits and vegetables in rainbow colors.

Buying a combination of fresh, frozen (if you have the freezer space), and canned and jarred fruits and veggies may be the best way to go.

Frozen fruits and vegetables may actually contain more nutrients than fresh ones, since certain nutrients begin to break down during the time it takes to transport, display, and sell the produce.

Flash-frozen fruits and vegetables are fantastic; the nutrients are instantly frozen in time and released when you thaw them.

Some canned foods—and foods in jars—actually have increased nutrients. The process includes heating them, and in some cases, heating releases antioxidants and other chemicals—which are very heart-friendly little guys. Also, sometimes nutrients are added to the food by the manufacturer.

There's also the matter of fresh vegetables just plain losing it while they're sitting around waiting for you to eat them!

How fast can a bowl of fresh peaches get fuzzy on you; how soon do those bananas spot up and get soft?

KEY WORDS TO LOOK FOR

KEY WORDS: WHOLE GRAIN, CALCIUM FORTIFIED, FORTIFIED, ENRICHED

Take advantage of these little words. They mean good things to you, especially in foods that are minimally processed.

> **F.Y.I.**
>
> "Wheat flour" isn't whole grain flour. "Whole wheat flour" is.

KEY WORDS: 100 PERCENT FRUIT JUICE

Drinks labeled "fruit juice drink," "fruit flavored drink," "fruit punch," or "fruitade" usually consist of water, water, and water, loads of sugar—and a small percentage of juice.

Check out the label—the law says it has to reveal the percentage of actual juice content. Five percent juice? Thirty-five percent juice? Go for the ones that say 100 percent juice.

If you want, you can take it home and stretch it by adding your own water and ice. Delicious!

KEY WORD: ORGANIC

The "organic" label means that the way the food/produce is grown complies with regulations set up by the government that define "organic"—which includes use of no genetically engineered seeds or crops, long-lasting pesticides, herbicides, or fungicides (bug and mold regulators) and no use of radiation during food processing.

They may not be as uniformly "perfect looking" as produce grown on giant farms, but oh so what! Who cares if an insect roosted on a plant and munched a teeny hole or two on a lettuce leaf before flying away?

> **F.Y.I.**
>
> Organic foods are optional—good, but not essential. Don't stress if your produce isn't organically grown.

KEY WORDS: LOW FAT

Good words in the dairy section—but not necessarily words that signal a nutritional advantage otherwise. Your goal is to **moderate** fat intake.

Fat-free? Why go there? Many fat-free products are loaded with sugar or refined carbs. And remember that good plant fats like olive, canola, soybean, corn, sesame, sunflower, or peanut oil can help you feel more satisfied with your meals.

KEY WORDS: PARTIALLY HYDROGENATED VEGETABLE OILS

These are trans fat tip-off words (see page 23). Trans fats lurk in large amounts in vegetable shortening, stick (hard) margarine, pound cake, and microwave popcorn. Okay occasionally, but try to minimize these.

Check the ingredients lists (see page 72).

THE CORNER STORE

Don't have access to a supermarket? Not everybody does. If your neighborhood convenience store or corner market is the only store close to where you live, you **can** shop there for nutritious food.

ADVOCATE!

If you don't find the foods you want, ask the storekeepers to start stocking them. Speak up. Let them know there is a demand!

THINK FOOD GROUPS
FRUIT GROUP

You might see apples and oranges, since they last a long time and the convenience store owner doesn't have to worry so much about their going bad before somebody—you, we hope—snaps them up.

Canned and dried fruit, including canned (or jarred) applesauce, is also good stuff—and it's usually available.

You'll also be able to locate canned fruit juice and bottled 100 percent fruit juice (especially apple juice) in the aisles and containers of cold 100 percent fruit juice in the refrigerator case. Remember: It's key that the juice be labeled 100 percent fruit **juice** (see page 67).

JIFFY LUNCH: LOW-FAT COTTAGE CHEESE AND FRUIT

How about canned fruit on top of low-fat cottage cheese for breakfast, lunch, or dinner? Cottage cheese is in the dairy case. If you can, choose fruit that's sweetened in its own juice rather than heavy syrup.

VEGETABLE GROUP

Convenience stores usually don't have many fresh vegetables. Sometimes you can find a few tomatoes or carrots and possibly a sad-looking head of lettuce.

Canned vegetables? If you like 'em, that's what counts. You should be able to find green beans and a few other veggies in cans. Go for low sodium. Or head for the low-sodium canned soups that have vegetables in 'em, like minestrone soup. Or get frozen vegetables instead. Some convenience stores have them!

Vegetable juice can be found in the cold drinks case—like V8, and that's a good choice.

Tomatoes are fantastic for you—full of vitamins, minerals, and heart-lovin' chemicals. Tomatoes can be found in lots of foods that are canned and jarred (low-sodium pizza sauce or pasta sauce).

Be on the lookout.

> Does a blob of ketchup count as a serving of vegetables? No, it doesn't—but ketchup still is fine for you as a taste booster because it contains our real nutritional starlet: tomato.

WHOLE GRAINS GROUP: BREAD, CEREAL, RICE, AND PASTA

Bread? If you have the choice, go for enriched whole grain bread. And you may be able to snag a box of multigrain or whole wheat crackers, preferably made without hydrogenated oils. See any whole grain tortillas?

Cereal? Cereal boxes that brag about being enriched or fortified on the front or back are a good bet as long as they're not loaded with added sugar. "Stone ground," "whole grain," and "high fiber" are also key words to find on the package.

A bowl of whole grain cereal with 1 percent low-fat or skim milk (and a little fresh or canned fruit thrown on top, when handy) is a universal fast meal. Or head for the (unsweetened) oatmeal. It's relatively inexpensive, easy to prepare, and will make you feel happily full.

Rice? Brown rice is whole grain and white isn't, but all rice is nice—and you probably won't find brown in a convenience store. Boxed white rice is usually enriched with vitamins and minerals. Go for it. Rice and (canned) beans are a delicious, nutritious combo. On your way out, why not ask the storekeeper to start stocking quick and convenient brown rice?

Pasta? Pasta is a good standby, especially whole grain pasta. As an alternative to tomato-based pasta sauce, frozen vegetables can be thrown together with pasta, olive oil, and grated Parmesan cheese.

PLANT OILS GROUP
Canola oil, olive oil, corn oil, peanut oil, sunflower oil, safflower oil, sesame seed oil, and soybean oil can probably be spotted.

LEAN ANIMAL PROTEIN GROUP: POULTRY, FISH, SEAFOOD, EGGS, AND LEAN RED MEAT
Sliced deli meats in plastic packets are often available in the refrigerated section; turkey and chicken are good choices. Check the expiration date to make sure these haven't expired before buying.

Eggs are in the dairy case. They're a great, affordable source of protein.

Have you ever eaten scrambled eggs topped with salsa, rolled up in a whole grain tortilla? If you're allowed to use the stove, try 'em this way.

NUTS AND BEANS (AND OTHER LEGUMES) GROUP
Canned beans abound. Hunt them down. Rinse before eating them to get rid of excess salt.

No convenience store is complete without nuts and sunflower seeds. Sunflower seeds are a great snack, but gosh—they're so little!

Nuts are usually found by the chips, in small packages near the cashier or on the ends of aisles. Expensive? Maybe. But they're more filling than chips and other snacks.

You'll also undoubtedly be able to locate peanut butter. More nuts for your bucks! Hopefully, you can find a jar that doesn't have partially hydrogenated oil listed in the ingredients.

How about canned lentil soup? A tasty and easy way to get your legumes.

LOW-FAT DAIRY GROUP

Hit the dairy case. There you will find 1 percent low-fat or skim milk, low-fat cottage cheese, low-fat cream cheese, low-fat or nonfat yogurt, and skim milk cheese (like string cheese).

Don't drink milk? Head to the juice case, where you will probably be able to find fruit juice that's marked "calcium fortified."

CANDY GROUP

Oh, sure.

A candy group.

Candy is right near the register, so we'll stare at it while we wait—and buy it on impulse.

Just like the magazine group!

Self-regulate. You're in charge.

chapter 12

FOOD LABELS/INGREDIENTS LISTS

As you stroll around the store, you may want to check out the food labels and ingredients lists on the packages of foods you're considering buying.

A little in-aisle, on-the-spot comparison shopping is a way of building your knowledge base.

WHAT'S UP WITH FOOD LABELS?

A food label, also known as a nutrition facts label, tells you information about the food that is considered extremely important from a nutritional standpoint.

DON'T NOODLE

No need to tally and count like a madwoman. If you find yourself obsessing over food labels, stop reading them.

Chill.

If you are following The Cactus Plan (see page 29) recommendations for three nutritious meals, (breakfast, lunch, and dinner) and a couple of healthy snacks in between, you'll be fine in the protein, carb, fat, vitamin, minerals, fiber, and calorie departments.

INGREDIENTS LIST

This is different from the nutrition facts label. The ingredients list tells you every last thing inside the package: E–V–E–R–Y–T–H–I–N–G. If you have food allergies, check the ingredients list on food packaging so you can know what foods to avoid.

By law, all of the ingredients in a package must be listed—and listed in a specific order. The first ingredient on the product's list must be the ingredient that there is most of by weight. Then the rest must follow in descending order by weight. The ingredients at the end of the list are the least abundant.

FOOD LABELS FOR BEGINNERS

Sometimes we casually check out food labels out of boredom while we are eating or drinking something.

Or we check 'em out after we're done.

At some point, you may want to pay closer attention to food labels, and if you do, keep in mind their purpose:

To help make sure we're getting enough nutrients and fiber—and not too much heart-unfriendly fat, cholesterol, or sodium.

> ## F.Y.I.
> ### STAY TUNED
> At the time of publication of this book, trans fat is not yet listed on all food labels . . . but it will be by January 2006.
>
> Currently, it's listed as **partially hydrogenated vegetable oil** on the ingredients list on food packaging.

LEARN IN STAGES

For now, just get a feel for the territory.

Understanding **daily value** is key: Daily value (DV) is the amount of each nutrient (and fiber) an adult would want to shoot for in a day, based on a 2,000-calorie plan. (For the purpose of learning to use food labels, you can pretend to be an adult.) It's based on percentages. One hundred percent in a day covers it for each category.

When you want to **increase** a nutrient or dietary fiber, go for foods with a DV of 20 percent or higher per serving.

When you want to **limit** something—like saturated fat, cholesterol, and sodium—go for foods that have 5 percent or less DV per serving.

> ## WHAT'S A SERVING?
> Five chips, ten chips, two cookies, twenty fish crackers?
>
> It depends!
>
> Check out the serving sizes and servings per container at the top of the label. But note that the serving size on a nutrition facts label may not be the same as a serving size in The Cactus Plan. For example, The Cactus Plan counts half a cup of pasta as a serving—but a nutrition facts label may count one cup of pasta as a serving.

Nutrition Facts

Serving Size 1 cup (228g)
Servings Per Container 2

Amount Per Serving

Calories 250   Calories from Fat 110

	% Daily Value*
Total Fat 12g	**18%**
Saturated Fat 3g	**15%**
Cholesterol 30mg	**10%**
Sodium 470mg	**20%**
Total Carbohydrate 31g	**10%**
Dietary Fiber 0g	**0%**
Sugars 5g	
Protein 5g	

Vitamin A	4%
Vitamin C	2%
Calcium	20%
Iron	4%

*Percent Daily Values are based on a 2,000-calorie diet. Your Daily Values may be higher or lower depending on your calorie needs:

	Calories:	2,000	2,500
Total Fat	Less than	65g	80g
Sat Fat	Less than	20g	25g
Cholesterol	Less than	300mg	300mg
Sodium	Less than	2,400mg	2,400mg
Total Carbohydrate		300g	375g
Dietary Fiber		25g	30g

(Remember: Checking out food labels is totally optional. But it can help you make better nutritional choices, become a smarter shopper, and get the most nutritional value out of the dollars you spend!)

WANT TO CHECK OUT CALCIUM, IRON, AND SATURATED FAT?

CALCIUM

Since calcium is such a key mineral for girls in the growth spurt, why not check food labels on dairy products, calcium-fortified orange juice, calcium-fortified soy and rice milk—and other packaged foods—to see how you're doing in the calcium department?

IRON

Yes, yes, yes. Girls do need iron, no doubt about it. And you can easily scout it out because many packaged foods are fortified with iron.

Food labels can help you figure out how to reach your goal of 100 percent. Check for iron listed on the label of, say, a ready-to-eat whole grain cereal box. If it says "Iron: 50%," it means one serving of the cereal would get you about halfway there.

SNACKS AND SATURATED FAT

Got the munchies?

Craving a little packaged something?

Choosing snacks with less than 5 percent DV of saturated fat (see page 23) per serving can contribute toward keeping your saturated fat intake in a healthy range over time.

As stated at the bottom of the Nutrition Facts label (page 74), at the level of 2,000 calories a day, no more than 20 grams (or 10% of calories) should come from SATU-RATED FATS. As a matter of fact, THE LESS SATURATED FATS THE BETTER!

Want to test your food label knowledge? Log on to **http://www.cfsan.fda.gov/label.html**

THE GOAL IS TO REACH 100 PERCENT DAILY VALUE (DV)

So here's how it works:

One glass of 1 percent low-fat or skim milk and one glass of calcium-fortified orange juice along with 1/4 cup of firm (calcium-set) tofu would satisfy the adult daily requirement, because 35 percent DV plus 35 percent DV plus 35 percent DV adds up to over 100 percent DV:

35 + 35 + 35 = 105

See? It's a math problem.

Actually, the calcium requirement of an adolescent girl is a little higher than for an adult under 50 years old. Yogurt, cheese, almond butter, white beans, sesame tahini, calcium-fortified foods and drinks, and (if recommended by your doctor) a calcium supplement can help you reach your daily goal (see page 15).

chapter 13

HOW GREAT IS THIS?

Physical activity can boost self-esteem, improve your self-image, lower stress, help relieve depression, reduce anxious feelings, get you out in the sunshine—and help keep your energy input and output in balance.

And more. **Sustained** (which means continuous) moderate to vigorous physical activity can do all of the above, plus strengthen your heart! See The Cactus Plan recommendations on page 29.

Remember that **weight-bearing** physical activity—activity that involves carrying weight (including the weight of your body)—can help build strong bones.

Being physically active can reduce your chances of developing health problems now and as an adult.

What kinds of problems? Now: **Obesity** (which is weighing way more than what's recommended for a person's height) and type 2 diabetes. Later: heart disease, brittle and weak bones, and certain kinds of cancers.

Yikes!

So what can you do?

ABOUT NOW

Physical activity helps you create and maintain a powerful presence: energy, strength, focus, athletic ability, confidence—and the sense of well-being and self-esteem you naturally acquire when your body operates at peak performance.

It helps you build and maintain a positive self-image and an upbeat attitude.

Being fit helps you perform better in school.

It also enables you to do physical work, play

sports, dance fast, exercise—and move your body from place to place without getting tired.

Training your body to function at more active levels makes it stronger and more productive during physical activity. It helps you build and maintain strong bones, muscles, and joints.

It helps improve balance, **agility** (the ability to move quickly with skill and control), power, reaction time, speed, and coordination.

BEING FIT IS FANTASTIC!

Physical activity includes play, dance, games, sports, house and yard cleaning, transporting yourself from place to place, recreation, PE—or other planned exercise in the context of family, school, and/or community activities.

Being physically active isn't a chore, and it's not something to get through, not something you assign yourself to do out of a sense of guilt.

The key is to identify ways of being active that you really look forward to, that you totally enjoy.

It's fun!

It feels good!

Those are the two best reasons to go for it!

Here's another one: **It keeps energy input in balance with energy output.**

To recap, energy output is about growth, metabolism, and physical activity.

Growth and metabolism just happen. Physical activity?

We have some guidelines for you.

THE CACTUS PLAN'S GUIDELINES FOR PHYSICAL ACTIVITY

REMINDER:

If you are extremely overweight or underweight or have other health considerations, talk to your doctor about personalizing an activity plan just for you—**before** you start (or change) your physical activity routine.

1. TRY TO PARTICIPATE IN PHYSICAL ACTIVITIES THAT ENABLE YOU TO ACCUMULATE (ADD UP) AT LEAST AN HOUR OR MORE OF "MODERATE" EXERCISE EVERY DAY.

You can estimate—loosely tally your time up during the course of the day.

Romping around outside, playing outdoor games and sports, participating in PE classes, shooting hoops, playing badminton, skateboarding, bicycling with your friends, walking briskly with a group of friends to school or the library or to a friend's house—all qualify (see "Safer in Numbers," page 87).

2. 3 DAYS OR MORE A WEEK, ABOUT 15–20 MINUTES OF YOUR HOUR (ABOVE) SHOULD BE SUSTAINED (CONTINUOUS) MODERATE TO VIGOROUS EXERCISE, WITH INTERMITTENT PERIODS OF REST AND RECOVERY.

Sustained (continuous) moderate to vigorous activity—stopping briefly now and then for rest and recovery—causes you to breathe harder, makes you sweat, and causes your heart to beat faster (see below).

You may need to work up to this goal slowly. And that's okay—in fact, it's the right way to begin. No pain, no gain? Wrong. There is no need for exercise to be painful.

ENJOYMENT IS ESSENTIAL

Figure out fun ways of being **really** active—activities that can get you breathing hard, make you sweat, and make your heart beat faster. These are called **vigorous** activities. It makes sense that if you love doing them, you'll be motivated to keep on doing them! This is especially true if you exercise with a friend or friends. Why not make exercising social whenever possible? It's more fun!

Dancing counts, so turn up the radio and dance with yourself in the mirror. So does jumping rope. (Double Dutch? How vigorous is that!) Playing tennis, soccer, and hockey; roller-skating and in-line skating; swimming laps; taking an aerobics class. What else?

You can figure this out.

You can!

Get back in touch with the little kid in you who loves to run and skip, jump and play.

TELL ME AGAIN: "SO WHAT'S THE PAYOFF?" YOU ASK

It's huge. Along with improving fitness, there's a laundry list of other benefits from being physically active:

CRAZY ~~EIGHT~~ GREAT PAYOFF LIST

1. Physical activity elevates the mood and relieves stress.

2. It's fun to be active—get in on it!

3. There are huge social perks—the potential to make new friends and spending time with friends are two of them.

4. You can learn and improve skills—very personally satisfying. And who knows how far you'll want to take it? A place on the team? An athletic scholarship to college? It happens all the time.

5. Staying in shape feels really good physically—which translates into feeling good all over.

6. Physical activity improves your appearance. How? Feeling really good is linked with looking your best.

7. You can increase your strength, endurance, and flexibility. This is fantastic for all sports—including noncompetitive

sports. An Olympic medal? Maybe it's in the stars for you. Don't count anything out.

8. You can keep your energy intake (calorie intake)/energy output in balance more easily when you are consistently physically active.

AND!

When you limit inactivity.

HUH?

Video games, TVs, computers, car pooling, riding the bus. What do these things have in common?

You guessed it: Sitting on the derriere.

The sorry fact is that we sit sit sit for hours and hours

and hours

and hours!

Every day.

We're not designed for this.

CHILLIN' LIKE A VILLAIN?

The Cactus Plan advises you to:

Limit TV watching (and screen time— meaning video game playing and computer use) to two hours a day.

UH???!?!?@?@#!??

Sorry, but if you stare at a screen for hours each day, you exercise your imagination less and spend less quality time with family and friends and less time developing your talents, interests, and intellect. And guess what.

Parking in front of a TV or computer for hours each day puts you at risk for becoming unfit.

Not moving around enough can cause you to lose flexibility, strength, and cardiovascular (heart) fitness over time. The goal is to gain flexibility and strength and endurance over time!

THE TV TRAP

Plus, when you're watching TV all day long, you're missing out on doing other activities that are more creative.

And personally satisfying.

And **esteem building,** which means feeling good about yourself.

So excessive TV viewing works against **mental** fitness.

It isn't satisfying for your spirit to fall into the TV trap, especially not now—at the time when your mind and body are all about growing and changing and exploring the world. Choose a couple of your favorite programs to watch alone or with your family—and skip the rest.

HERE'S THE KICKER

Humans are designed to move throughout the day. That's what's natural.

Watching TV throws off your balance regarding your intake of food (calories) and your natural output of energy.

1. Lounging around in front of the TV uses way less energy than doing just about **anything** else (except sleeping, maybe).

2. Not only are you not moving (unless you count an occasional blink), but you might just also be mindlessly turbo snacking.

3. While you are watching TV, your food choices are being influenced by lots of bogus ads.

Certain food advertisements have the goal of getting us to eat larger quantities than we want or need, to eat more often than we want or need, and to eat when we're not hungry.

Ads often feature beautiful, popular people grubbing gargantuan feasts of fast food dressed with mayo and slugging down soft drinks by the gallons—as if we could (and should) be doing this 24/7.

AS IF

It goes without saying that this approach to marketing has everything to do with $$$$$, may have little to do with nutrition, and is completely idiotic. But you've got a brain and can use it.

SPEAKING OF WHICH . . .

Sure, it's fun to just veg out sometimes in front of the TV. But sometimes it's good to elevate the level of the info.

Public broadcasting stations (PBS) have programs that challenge your dome and have no ads.

Documentary films, wildlife programs, programs about books and music and art and science and history and geography and geology can be so fascinating.

How about tuning in to a cooking show and watching it with your parent? Get out that pencil and paper. You'll learn about cooking and get great new ideas for meals and snacks.

Maybe you and your parent will see something so scrumptious, you'll be inspired to add the ingredients to your shopping list and make immediate plans to cook it together!

Remember: You're growing intellectually, which is all about your ability to think, reason, and understand. TV can be part of that process when you bump it up a notch or two.

DENIAL IS A RIVER IN EGYPT

So be honest with yourself. About how long are you spending watching TV every day?

Estimate.

Once you confront the true time factor, you (and only you) can make a necessary adjustment.

Set some limits for yourself.

You can!

chapter 14

ALL THE RIGHT MOVES

GETTING IT STRAIGHT

Okay. So *physical activity* is "any bodily movement produced by skeletal muscles that results in energy expenditure." This includes things you do all day long—going up and down stairways, walking into the bathroom, and even brushing your teeth.

Exercise is "any kind of physical activity that is planned, structured, or repetitive." So exercise is also physical activity. But it includes stuff like jumping rope for five minutes straight or taking a few laps around the track to get your heart beating faster—on purpose.

Physical fitness is a set of attributes (characteristics) that is either *health related* or *skill related*.

Health-related fitness includes cardiovascular endurance, muscular strength and endurance, and flexibility and body composition.

Skill-related fitness includes balance, agility, power, reaction time, speed, and coordination. These skills improve as we participate in physical activities like games, sports (both noncompetitive and competitive), exercise programs, and recreational (for pleasure and relaxation) physical activities.

> **REMEMBER:**
>
> If your weight seems to be an obstacle to your moving around easily and/or comfortably, make a physical activity plan with your doctor before starting to exercise.

LET'S GO!

Being fit involves paying attention to three kinds of exercise: healthy heart (cardiovascular) endurance, muscle strength, and *F-L-E-X-I-B-I-L-I-T-Y.*

HEADS UP! To avoid injury, check out the warm-up/cooldown exercises on pages 84 and 85.

EXERCISING AND WORKING OUT

Physical activity is about movement, and exercise is one brand of movement. Think of exercise as planned physical activity.

The number-one rule for exercising is: Pace yourself. Maintain a comfortable speed so that you can perform your exercise over an extended period.

And keep in mind that even a moderate workout requires a warm-up, stretch, cooldown, and cooldown stretch.

Warming up is the first part of a safe workout. Warming up helps prevent injuries, increases your body temperature, and "softens" the muscles and gets the body ready for the rest of the workout.

You can warm up by doing a series of slow movements for five or ten minutes; slowly jog in place or do jumping jacks, for example.

Stretching improves flexibility fitness, improves the body's ability to move, and decreases the number of injuries related to physical activity.

It's important to use proper form to avoid injuries while stretching. Ask your PE teacher, coach, health care professional, or other qualified adult to demonstrate safe stretching form and techniques **before** you begin stretching.

Safe stretching involves understanding proper form and that you should NOT go beyond comfortable levels, that it's important to stretch s-l-o-w-l-y, that you should hold the stretch **gently** (for about ten seconds), and that you should **not bounce**.

Cooling down lets the body slow down and recover from the fitness activity and helps prevent soreness (and injury). Cool down by walking slowly or walking slowly in place.

Cooldown stretches help prevent soreness and improve fitness flexibility.

Yoga and tai chi are other great ways to stretch as well! Check one out when a family member or friend goes to their next class.

FLEXIBILITY FITNESS

The ability of muscles and joints to flex is called *flexibility fitness.*

Your muscles need to move and stretch through a full range of motions. When you're "flexibly fit," you're less likely to get hurt during physical activity.

Increase your flexibility! Stretch those muscles so that they stay flexible enough to support your joints.

Check out the stretching exercises on the following two pages.

Improve flexibility fitness by combining stretching with aerobics!

EXAMPLES OF STRETCHES YOU CAN LEARN HOW TO DO WITH HELP FROM A QUALIFIED INSTRUCTOR

Remember: It's important to use proper form to avoid injuries while stretching. The extent of stretching depends on your flexibility! Ask your PE teacher, coach, health care professional, or other qualified adult to demonstrate safe stretching form and techniques **before** you begin.

Safe stretching involves understanding how **NOT to go beyond comfortable levels,** how to stretch **s-l-o-w-l-y**, how to hold the stretch **gently** (for about ten seconds), and that **you should NOT bounce.**

PALMS TO CEILING

BUTTERFLY

NECK STRETCH

ARMS AND SHOULDERS STRETCH

QUAD BURNER

REACH BACK

WAVE

LOWER LEG STRETCH

Rent an exercise video, borrow one from the library, or join a class at your local Y, Boys and Girls Club, church, or community center. Aerobics classes are a great place to make new friends.

Or bring your parent along!

FITNESS CLOTHES

Hmmm. Tights and belly shirts? Do we actually need to wear such things when we exercise?

Keep in mind that the fashion industry sometimes connects with the fitness industry to create the illusion that we need to LOOK a certain way before we work out. Why?

To sell stuff!

Working out feels good and is good for you mentally, emotionally, and physically. Those are the reasons to do it.

Don't stress over what you are wearing or how you look when you move, bend, dance, reach, or jump.

Worrying so much about **how you look** that it prevents you from working out is totally counterproductive.

Don't do this to yourself!

GET COMFORTABLE

A magazine ad portrays a model out in the great outdoors with her friends. She's wearing, perhaps, a pair of microshorts—and maybe a sturdy pair of rubber flip-flops?

Let's get real, folks.

When exercising, dress appropriately. Consider the temperature so you don't get too hot (or cold). Wear comfortable underwear (cotton is best) and a sports bra that hugs your breasts close to your chest if you need one. Throw a shirt over it and put on some sweats or other loose-fitting pants or shorts, socks—and shoes appropriate for the activity.

Tie a sweatshirt around your waist if it's chilly out.

Leave it at that.

LET'S NOT PRETEND

It would be just so great if you could walk, hike, jog, in-line skate, skateboard, or ride a bike or scooter whenever and wherever you want to without being at risk of harm.

But let's not kid ourselves; you can't.

EXERCISE YOUR OPTIONS!

You can find so many fun ways to be active that are safe and supervised—so start looking! Explore your options at school in PE or in after-school programs, in classes at your local Y or Boys and Girls Club, or in other **supervised** programs for kids sponsored by your city, county, state, religious group, or other community or government organization.

SAFER IN NUMBERS

If your parent says it's okay for you to exercise in your neighborhood or walk to school with your friends, fine—but stay alert and aware of your surroundings. You're safer in numbers, but you still have to stay on top of things! Stick to the route you've agreed on.

Don't get sidetracked.

SAFETY TIPS

• Avoid taking shortcuts through alleys, parking lots, wooded areas, creek beds, railroad tracks, or other out-of-the-way places.

• Leave your portable music players at home so you can hear approaching vehicles (and people) and so you won't zone out on the music.

• Wear something bright so you'll be visible from a distance. Don't exercise outside at dusk or at night.

• If you can, bring a cell phone along. If someone poses a threat to you or your friends, call 911 or the police emergency number without delay. And keep track of your surroundings so you can immediately tell them where you are.

• Trust your instincts! Fear is a powerful guide. If something **seems** "off" about a person or a situation, it *is* "off." Stay on your toes.

• If a car, van, or truck pulls up close or stops close to you and your friends, all stand way back. Don't interact with the driver or a passenger. Be ready to run.

• The opposite direction that the car is heading is often your best retreat because it takes time for the car to turn around.

• Don't be tricked. Don't interact with someone you don't know well. Acquaintances, not just strangers, can pose a threat to kids.

BUMMER

It's a total drag that kids can't depend on being safe in the world.

But do keep in mind that there's lots you can do to minimize your risks. Being alert and prepared to act definitely helps keep you safer.

It also puts out a vibe: Don't mess with me and my friends.

ENDURANCE/CARDIOVASCULAR (HEALTHY HEART) FITNESS

Your heart needs to deliver in lots of different ways.

At rest, it needs to beat at a slow, steady pace and pump lots of blood with each beat so that oxygen and nutrients can be carried through your blood vessels to every area of your body. When your heart is strong, it works more efficiently. You can move faster and work and play harder for longer periods without getting tired and wanting to quit.

Endurance fitness helps improve your heart muscle, your lungs, and your blood vessels.

BUILD YOUR ENDURANCE THROUGH AEROBIC EXERCISE

Aerobic exercise is about air. It's about breathing hard, moving fast, sweating, and having your heart beat faster.

A reasonable goal is to find a pace (speed) that you can do continuously for about 15–20 minutes, with brief periods for rest and recovery. Pace, don't race. See page 78 and The Cactus Plan (on page 29) for more specific recommendations. **Weight or health concerns? First talk to your doctor about tailoring a physical activity plan just for you.**

SWEAT

Sweating is a good thing; in fact, it's essential. It cools your body and keeps your temperature in a healthy range.

THE FLUID FACTOR

It's especially important to drink water when you're exercising hard. Your body sweats to cool itself. Fluids are lost that need to be replaced.

Drink water before, during, and after vigorous exercise (see pages 9 and 31).

(see pages 9 and 31)

HEADS UP!

Apartment/building stairwells are **not** safe places to exercise alone. The recommendation to "take the stairs instead of the elevator" doesn't apply in your situation. Stay safe!

Have stairs in your house? They can be your stationary StairMaster. Climb them a few times.

Limited space? Try jumping jacks. Get out that jump rope! How fun is it to skip rope to music!

Like to dance? Go for it.

Dancing also totally improves your coordination.

DANCING IS UNIVERSAL!

Are there traditional dances that are a part of your culture—or a friend's?

Native American dance, hip-hop, Greek dance, Chinese dance, salsa, Irish dance, African dance, Russian dance. What culture **doesn't** dance?

Celebrate your cultural heritage!

Look into possibilities in your community.

LOVIN' YOUR HEART

Like every other muscle, with exercise your heart can grow stronger. You improve the endurance of your heart by getting it to beat faster through vigorous aerobic exercise.

AEROBIC IS ABOUT OXYGEN (AIR)

Aerobic exercise is the exercise that helps your heart the most.

When you're physically fit, more blood is pumped with each heartbeat, and so your heart can beat more slowly at rest and beat more efficiently during vigorous physical activity.

With a healthy heart, you're able to do more physical activity (and work) for longer periods before becoming tired.

Why?

Because your heart will be very efficiently getting oxygen to all areas of your body, including your muscles—which need plenty of oxygen to keep on working.

And stop to think about it: Your heart is a muscle, and when it's healthy, it's delivering plenty of oxygen to itself!

HEADS UP!

Undereating and overexercising is a dangerous combination; it puts your heart at risk. Eat well. Enjoy exercising. Don't take it to extremes.

If you have a friend who seems to be **overexercising,** tell an adult.

MIGHTY BONES WITH EXERCISE!

Besides having enough calcium, weight-bearing exercise is very important to build your bones and keep them strong.

Hike.

Walk.

Climb stairs.

Play badminton, basketball, soccer, or tennis.

Jump rope.

And dance!

Go for it!!

F.Y.I.

Find out more about powerful bones, powerful girls at

http://www.cdc.gov/powerfulbones

http://www.cdc.gov/nccdphp/dnpa/
bonehealth/bonehealth.htm

VIGOROUS PHYSICAL ACTIVITY

Playing soccer, playing basketball, playing Ping-Pong, and numerous other activities are considered vigorous.

Rent a workout video or DVD, borrow an aerobic video or DVD from the library, or join a class at your local Y, Boys and Girls Club, church, or community center.

Or swim!

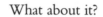

HAVE FUN!

Many communities have a YWCA or other public facility where you can take swimming lessons taught by a certified swimming instructor (through a Red Cross or YWCA certified program) and swim for a reasonable fee.

Swimming is just **such** great exercise. It's *low impact:* easy on the joints. Since you're supported by water, there's less chance of injury—compared to "land" sports.

When you swim, you use almost every major muscle group in your body, and if you swim long distances, you'll get fantastic aerobic exercise that will improve your cardiovascular endurance. Playing games in the water with your friends and family helps keep you fit—because it keeps you moving!

Best of all, swimming and playing in the water is completely relaxing and fun.

Why not call around? Start with your city's parks and recreation department.

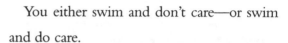

BUT WHAT ABOUT MY HAIR!

What about it?

You either swim and don't care—or swim and do care.

But you don't let the bother of it keep you from swimming.

If you have long hair, after you dip, be ready to smack some conditioner in it, wrap it up in a ponytail, and call it a day.

Or wrestle your hair into a bathing cap before your dunk.

Your healthy, invigorated, after-swim look will cancel out any perceived hair (or makeup) probs.

CHLORINE

Pool water has chlorine in it to zap germs. After a swim, your skin and hair will like it better if you take a moment to rinse your beautiful self off in the shower—head to toe.

And special shampoos for coping with chlorine?

Look into it.

COMMIT TO BEING ACTIVE AND GO WITH THE FLOW

Refuse to allow minor fashion details to get in the way of your physical activity—which de-stresses you and builds confidence and self-esteem. And tones your muscles.

And puts sparkles in your eyes!

That's way more magnetic than mascara!

Physical activity can make you feel great, and how you feel shows.

Feeling good physically can be your biggest asset.

It's part of the message you're capable of putting out in the world:

It's great to be alive!

SAFETY TIPS

Don't swim alone, even if you're a good swimmer.

There should always be somebody in or near the pool while you dip, dunk, and swim—in case you bump your head or have another health emergency.

Swim where there are lifeguards.

Dive only from the end of a diving board into deep water where you can clearly see the bottom.

If you get tired while you're swimming or get a cramp—don't panic. Just roll onto your back and float—slowly kicking to the nearest edge or to shallow water.

GET READY TO MAKE SOME WAVES AT YOUR SCHOOL

Speak up!

You know that being physically active can help you (and everybody else) maintain better self-esteem and lower levels of stress and anxiety. Get some friends together and speak as a group.

Ask for resource support ($$$$$$$$$ and trained supervision) for school-based intra-mural sports programs and physical activity clubs, like aerobics clubs, dance clubs, hiking clubs, bike-riding clubs—whatever seems to fit your school environment.

And while you're at it, ask that your school have daily PE classes that are fun and varied with activities that can be carried on throughout your lives. Bowling, bicycling, swing dancing—even kayaking—are included in PE activity in some schools.

Why not yours?

NO ROOM FOR STUDENTS WHO AREN'T VERY "ATHLETIC" IN PE CLASSES?

If this is true in your school, ask a parent, teacher, or doctor to have a little chat with the coach or principal. Is anybody's parent a health care professional who could go to bat for you? All schools should offer diverse, fun physical activities that take into consideration the fact that students have different levels of athletic abilities (and interest).

Less athletic, overweight, or obese (see page 76) students should NOT be shut out of routine physical activity opportunities during PE at school.

No way!

HATE SPORTS?

Lots of people do, so join the club. Still, be active. Noncompetitive physical activities that stress participation rather than winning are great ways to go. How about suggesting a supervised "extended recess" program where you have a blast playing kickball, dodgeball, steal the bacon, and other fun games you played back in the day . . . when you were a little twerp?

> Want to find out more about staying physically active? Log on to VERB, at
>
> http://www.verbnow.com

STRENGTH/RESISTANCE FITNESS

Strength fitness improves the ability of your muscles to move or resist a force or workload. It helps you perform your daily tasks without getting pooped. Moderate exercise that involves using your muscles can improve your strength fitness. Strong muscles lead to strong bones.

Strength/resistance training refers to the amount of work and time your muscles can perform (lift, pull, push, carry, etc.) before getting tired. It helps prevent injuries and improves your skills in games and sports—including jumping rope and shooting baskets.

DON'T ATTEMPT WEIGHT LIFTING WITHOUT THE ADVICE OF A TRAINED PROFESSIONAL

You can build up your strength fitness by going faster, going longer, lifting heavier objects, exercising more often—but you can also injure yourself doing any of these things too strenuously, too rapidly, or in the wrong positions.

Does your coach, PE teacher, or health care professional have information for you? Check it out.

Remember: Train—don't strain—and don't do too much, too soon.

Build muscles slowly.

Regular, modest weight training is the way to go.

YAKKITY YAK—DON'T TALK BACK!

Very few people want to spend their spare time doing chores. But somebody has to do 'em!

Chores can involve combinations of lifting (which improves strength), reaching (which improves flexibility), and aerobic (cardiovascular) exercise—which improves endurance and keeps your heart healthy and strong.

First, put on some music. It's easy (well, easier, anyway) to be a merry maid . . . with a good sound track behind you.

FOR ALL THE WAYS YOU PLAY

Little sisters and brothers in the house? Big sisters influence their peeps. Be a role model.

Romp and play with them!

Playful daily shenanigans tame the wild beast!

(Including if the wild beast happens to be you.)

chapter 15

A BEAUTIFUL PRESENCE

You're in the process of evolving into an adult and establishing your own way of being in the world.

Your outlook, thoughts, words, and actions have such great potential for contributing positively.

BEAUTY IS DEFINED IN SO MANY WAYS

And it definitely doesn't refer exclusively to physical characteristics. Universally, there are few people considered more attractive than those who are self-assured and considerate, avoid judging others—and who notice (and help bring out) the best in other people.

A GREAT VIBE

Having a beautiful presence—a great vibe—includes having a positive attitude toward yourself and others.

Being kind, caring, intuitive, and able to get along with others; having a sense of inner strength; being able to bounce back; being real, spontaneous, creative, inspired, peaceful, connected, in touch with the present, conscious of nature, evolving . . . these are characteristics that can be associated with having a great vibe.

TRUST

A powerful, positive vibe obviously doesn't include betraying confidences and hurting others when they are **vulnerable** (when they are open to harm).

Being someone whom other people trust puts you in a position of honor, responsibility, power, and respect.

APPROACH LIFE INTELLIGENTLY

Read.

Listen to music.

Go to school.

Arrive on time, well rested and well nourished so your brain can stay focused and operate at peak performance.

Listen to other people, read, think things through for yourself, and express your point of view.

BE CLASSY

Interact caringly with the people around you.

Be aware that things you say and do are making a statement about who you are.

Does your school have any supervised community-based volunteer programs that are open to youth participation? Check it out!

KEEP IT POSITIVE

Focusing too much on physical appearance can get in the way of normal development into a confident, productive adult.

You're a person, valued most for your inner qualities—like wisdom, honesty, integrity, loyalty, creativity, determination, compassion, and courage. Develop your interests, talent, and intellect—the things that **really** relate to success, style, accomplishment, and power.

Value these qualities in yourself!

Power, beauty, excitement, and sensuality arise from feelings of good health, high energy, physical fitness, self-esteem, and self-confidence.

THINK ABOUT IT

If you often comment on other people's appearance, you give the impression that you have a superficial view of others; this is no way to make (or keep) friends.

Have an opinion on somebody's size or shape? Save it.

And while you're at it, show respect for yourself. If you are saying and thinking negative things about your physical appearance, you may end up believing them. And convincing others that they're true.

BODY IMAGE

Body size and shape are two small parts of an incredibly complex and beautiful package: you.

PEOPLE ARE VARIED. WE'RE SUPPOSED TO BE.

Imagine if everybody looked and acted the same. How boring would that be? Celebrate your unique characteristics and those of the people around you.

The color of your eyes, the texture of your hair, the shade of your skin, the shape of your body—all of these things were determined before you were born.

MAINTAINING A POSITIVE, HEALTHY ATTITUDE TOWARD YOUR CHANGING BODY IS SO IMPORTANT!

It is just **not** okay for anyone—and we mean **anyone**—to make comments or behave in a way that makes you feel uncomfortable about your body. If this happens to you, tell an adult you trust.

HEADS UP!

Is someone outside of your same age group (an older teen or adult) expressing a romantic interest in you?

This is *not* okay. And it's *not* your "fault."

Say no and talk to your parent or another adult you trust about it.

BODY IMAGE AND SPORTS

Certain sports have the potential of stressing out young athletes by overly emphasizing weight and body type.

Gymnasts?

No, you will NOT maintain the body of a little kid.

You're not supposed to!

Who knows what size you'll naturally be once you go through your growth spurt? You are not a pixie—you're a person, a young woman athlete.

There are lots of sports that demand strength, flexibility, concentration, and balance **and** honor (and value) our naturally beautiful wide range of body types.

Calling All Ballerinas!

Is having the "perfect" ballerina's body just getting to be too much for you to stand? If so, tell your parent, teacher, coach.

BREAK THE MOLD!

Insist that a wider range of body types be accepted by your dance group or troupe.

What? Bigger girls can't dance?

What total rubbish is that?

NO LUCK?

There are many ways of dancing that show-case and express your creativity and talent without running the risk of sabotaging your self-esteem. Explore your options.

A SENSE OF STYLE

You're born with certain looks, but you create your own style. Be original. You are about you. So don't measure yourself against other girls.

Developing a unique presence and sense of style happens over time, not overnight. It begins with the realization that appearance is more than just how you look and that style is more than appearance.

Your sense of style can involve fashion that expresses and makes a statement about you. Fashion is an incredible, wonderful vehicle for expressing the emerging you! Choose clothing because you love the look, because it expresses the inner you. Don't limit yourself.

Don't restrict your fashion choices because your body doesn't happen to look like a model's body.

Express yourself!

GET IT GOING ON!

Love the creative aspects of fashion; put together outfits that you like to move in. Express yourself with fashion—don't limit yourself with it!

SECONDHAND ROSE

Thrift stores and secondhand stores shouldn't be overlooked.

Any hand-me-downs available in your family from the older generation? Styles generally make an encore appearance every twenty years. Vintage is cool because everything has a story.

What's in the way, way back of your grandma's closet?

Ask her if you can take a look.

MEDIA LITERACY

Media literacy is about being skilled at understanding the information being presented in newspapers, magazines, and books and on radio, TV, and the Internet. It's about being able to sort out what is reliable, what is true, whether or not there is a hidden agenda behind the information—and if there is, how to identify it.

Understanding how advertising works is one step toward becoming media literate.

MARKETING SPECIFICALLY TO TEENS

Companies who sell goods and services aggressively market to kids through ads and TV commercials because kids and teens spend gazillions of dollars on products.

There's plenty of misinformation headed your way, neatly packaged in ads that appeal to your age group.

ADS IN DISGUISE

In a romantic movie, a starlet steps out on the balcony and lights a cigarette. A total hottie sees her through the window. He strolls out to join her.

They stand there, gazing out at the twinkling city lights below them—saying nothing. Just standing in the moonlight.

It's a cigarette ad.

JUST SO YOU KNOW . . .

Here's a partial list of products that are presently aggressively marketed to you:

TVs

VCRs

DVDs

Clothing

Sneakers

Cosmetics

Video games

Hair products

Fitness equipment

Sodas

Fitness clothing

Cell phones

Weight-loss products

Fitness gimmicks

Fast food/convenient food/candy

AND . . .

Alcohol (fizzy, sweet alcoholic drinks)

Tobacco (cigarettes)

How irresponsible is that?

YOU'RE NOT GOOD ENOUGH?

Yes, you are.

But one basic goal of advertising is to make you believe, somehow, that your life will be better if you buy the product that's being advertised. Or that you need to change.

To improve!

While watching commercials or checking out magazine ads, it's important to identify just whose interests are being served.

Ask yourself: What is being advertised here? What strategy is being used to convince me to buy it? Do I really need it? Is it actually good for me?

ADS THAT ENCOURAGE PREOCCUPATION WITH THE BODY

Certain companies associated with the diet, fitness, and fashion industries make a huge profit by getting people to link food and fitness with **appearance**—rather than with optimum health and peak performance.

THINK ABOUT IT...

Energy output happens through growth, metabolism, and physical activity—you know this. There is nothing that people can eat or drink that burns fat.

"Fat burner" products like all "quick weight loss" powders, pills, and herbal potions *are a complete scam.*

Some are dangerous.

Don't buy or use them.

KEEP IT REAL

People are genetically programmed to be a variety of body types. Fitness ads, especially those featured in teen or fashion magazines, are famous for portraying unrealistic images of both women and men.

Achieving the supposedly "perfect" body is not a meaningful goal. Accepting ourselves and each other, including our different body types, is!

> ### F.Y.I.
>
> Photos of models in ads are often enhanced—which means faked. The photo's touched up.
>
> Many models have had breast enlargement surgery, tummy tucks, rear lifts, rib removal. Pretty brutal things to do for no medical reason, wouldn't you say?

Having the goal of achieving the body type pushed by the media and the fashion and fitness industries can really get in the way of your healthy development.

Don't sacrifice your health and energy to perform well for the sake of fulfilling somebody else's shallow definition of beauty.

Stay focused. Don't get stuck! Stick with The Cactus Plan, get enough sleep, nourish your body with healthy eating, and stay active. You will be where you want to be.

> ### JUST SAY NO
>
> If certain magazines make you feel crummy about yourself, hey—don't read them!

DUMMIES?

Girls are regularly portrayed in fashion ads as silly, mindless puffs of fluff whose main job is to look babyish and relatively dopey and to be weak and nonthreatening, and whose only goal is to reel in and land a cute boy.

The sorry fact is that these ads are totally off base. Girls rock.

REGULATE

You and your friends and classmates can have an effect on irresponsible advertising.

Suggest to your teacher or youth group leader that she or he sponsor a contest to find who can bring in the best and worst ads targeting kids.

Ask that a few minutes at the beginning of each meeting be reserved for discussing and evaluating the ads kids bring in.

To keep it cool for school, limit ads to those found in teen magazines or magazines you could find in the public library.

After the contest, have a letter-writing campaign to influence the companies (and magazines) sponsoring the worst ads.

A POSITIVE SPIN ON THE CONTEST

Do make sure to include great ads in the mix. Then write those companies to signal your total approval!

Advertising responsibly for legitimate, useful, helpful products, services, and organizations is a powerful way to make a positive impact on the world. Ever consider a career in advertising?

PUBLIC INTEREST ADS

Reality check: Smoking does **NOT** make people slim, popular, romantic, or powerful. It's an expensive, useless, smelly addiction that—among other things—interferes with athletic performance and causes bad breath, stained teeth, gum disease, and potentially fatal illnesses like cancer and heart and lung disease. Maybe your class could develop an ad campaign against smoking for your school.

YOU CAN MAKE A DIFFERENCE!

chapter **16**

YOU, THE AMAZING YOU

The love of your family and friends, sunlight, water, the good things food contains—along with your natural ability to physically experience the world—will help support your healthy physical, intellectual, and emotional growth as you continue becoming an adult.

YOUR BUDS

During puberty, friendships become more central in your life. Shopping, snacking, eating meals, preparing food together, exercising together—these are great ways to spend time with your friends.

BRANCHING OUT

As you experience more independence, you can take advantage of your community's resources. You can become more active in school, more able to advocate for yourself and your friends. You'll reach out and discover that the world is full of people who care about each other and that your future is full of promise and possibilities.

PEOPLE NEED PEOPLE

Feel the love.

PEOPLE NEED NATURE

Experiencing nature can give you a reassuring sense of place in the universe. You were born into this world; you're a part of this place.

FOR SURE

You belong.

YOUR ROOTS

Your relationship with your parents and family is changing, evolving.

You're becoming more independent.

This doesn't mean you have to separate from your parents and adult caregivers, though.

That's a myth.

Being connected to your family and culture is about as basic as it gets.

RELATE

Look to your parents for support and advice.

Separating isn't the issue; understanding and defining your changing roles is.

There's a wide range of parenting styles. Honor and value your own family's approach to parenting as you negotiate change in your relationship.

Make time for your parents, peeps, and grandparents. Maintaining strong family ties that span generations gives a powerful message to the world: You are loved and cared about.

BUT CAN THEY MAKE TIME FOR YOU?

Parents can get into quite the frenzy as they attempt to juggle a wide range of commitments and responsibilities.

So you may need to actually schedule a time when you can get your parent's undivided attention so you can discuss your concerns, viewpoint—or whatever.

No, it's not always a bed of roses. And yes, conflicts do come up in all family relationships.

YOU CAN WORK IT OUT

Human emotional and intellectual development is a lifelong process. Your parents are continuing to develop emotionally and intellectually. They're growing with you and sometimes find themselves in uncharted territory.

FAMILY COUNSELING

Your parents may not always parent skillfully or wisely, perhaps because of difficulties that they may have encountered or are now experiencing.

If communication isn't as good as you'd like it to be between you and your parents, it might be best for your family to get help from a mental health care professional.

Talk to your pediatrician, school counselor, school nurse, or other health care professional about what options are available to help your family grow stronger—together.

THE STRESS FACTOR

Nurturing the inner you is tied into taking care of your physical self.

Managing stress and identifying when you need to reach out for help with the emotional part of you are also key. It's stressful to grow up—no doubt about it.

How do you reduce stress?

Physical activity may be number one, coupled with getting enough sleep.

Breathing exercises, listening to music, singing, playing music, expressing yourself with writing or art and (for some people) yoga, tai chi, prayer, and/or meditation, and spending time outdoors with nature are helpful for stress reduction.

Stressed to the max? For a long time? Ask your health care professional to refer you to a counselor.

You've just got to build some downtime into your busy schedule! You really can do this—and will be so happy and relieved to have saved a peaceful place in your life.

TALK

Talking about painful, overwhelming, unhappy feelings—like sadness, anxiety, fear, frustration, and loneliness—with someone you trust and love can reduce stress and make the feelings less painful.

It also builds strong, healthy family relationships.

It's good to rely on your parents for emotional support and comfort. Hang out with your parents and other family. They love you and know you the best.

But your friends know you and care about you, too!

They can be there for you.

YOU CAN BE THERE FOR YOU

Certain ways of thinking can cast a shadow on your sunny outlook. You may need to remind yourself that:

1. Something that isn't quite perfect is NOT a total failure.

2. If something goes wrong, it doesn't mean that *everything* will go wrong.

3. Your accomplishments and positive qualities do too count. Acknowledge and appreciate them.

4. Without evidence to back up your conclusions, it would be better that you don't assume the worst. There may be positives you're not acknowledging because you're so stressed!

5. You don't have a crystal ball, so don't predict things will turn out badly. Assume things will work out; if they don't, deal with it.

6. Exaggerating your shortcomings and problems—and at the same time minimizing your positive qualities? How unfair is that? Give yourself a break.

7. We all make mistakes. You are not the same as what you do. Don't label yourself as a loser. It may not seem like it, but mistakes can be great for teaching us to do things differently.

8. Things don't always have the outcome we wish and hope for. Some situations are hard to accept, but eventually you will feel happier. Do think of the good side whenever possible.

9. Things are continuously changing—including feeling low. Remember that your outlook will brighten!

10. Having a problem with someone? Try to see how you may have also contributed to the problem—and at the same time, see how others involved may have contributed.

Take responsibility—but don't take responsibility for things that you're not responsible for.

RELATIONAL BULLYING

Relational bullying is bullying by "friends."

Basically, it's about making up lies, spreading rumors, betraying trust, and dumping people for no apparent reason. Who does this to friends?

Power is not about aggression, but relational bullying is. What's cool about it?

Nothing.

Be part of the solution, not part of the problem. Don't reinforce the behavior of bullies by showing or saying you agree.

Someone at school being bullied? Report it to a trusted adult.

ASK FOR HELP WHEN YOU NEED IT

You do have the power to help improve your moods, but you might need help to do this in the best way possible.

Not all troublesome feelings or conflicts can be resolved by talking about them with your family and friends.

Not all can be resolved by thinking positively, either.

If you are experiencing sad, worried, angry, or anxious feelings that don't go away or keep coming back again, ask for help. If your emotions or behaviors seem out of control, ask for help. If you are suffering from a traumatic event, ask for help.

Just about every community has mental health care available for children and teens who need help—including help with anger, anxiety, depression, and eating disorders (see page 106).

Mental health care may include *therapy* and/or medication.

HOW TO GET THE BALL ROLLING

A physician, pediatrician, or other health care provider can give you a referral to a mental health professional. Talk to your parent, your school counselor, your school nurse, or another responsible, reliable adult about helping you find professional mental heath care in your area. Your county health department (listed in government listings under County Government Offices in the front of the phone book) has a children's mental health division. In an emergency, call 911 or the police emergency number for your area. Also: See Hotlines on page 107.

THERAPY

Therapy is a process that involves talking, listening, and having a trained professional really, **really** listen to you!

With guidance, you can identify and explore what's making you feel bad and work through the problem. As the problem is resolved, positive thoughts and good feelings will begin to replace the negative, sad ones.

It isn't necessary to feel sad, scared, anxious, or "out of control" to get counseling or help. Lots of people talk to mental health care professionals to get ideas about themselves—understand themselves—and improve coping skills.

Getting therapy doesn't mean you're crazy or can't help yourself. It enables you to understand your life better and feel more in control of it. A counselor can help guide you as you discover new possibilities, ID your dreams, and set goals for yourself that you **can** accomplish!

HEADS UP!

If you have extremely anxious feelings about food, physical activity, and/or body image, talk to your parent and definitely make an appointment to talk to a counselor.

Sometimes (*not* always) these feelings can be related to the development of an **eating disorder.**

The behaviors associated with eating disorders are physically, emotionally, and mentally harmful and can become life-threatening if not treated.

Anorexia and *bulimia* are the names for two eating disorders that you may have read about in newspapers or magazines.

JUST DON'T GO THERE

It's unhealthy and dangerous to try to control weight by intentionally interfering with the body's natural process of metabolizing food and fluids. These behaviors may put the person at risk for developing an eating disorder or may indicate that the person already has one.

Also: Drugs that dehydrate the body or speed up the normal process of eliminating waste are sometimes improperly used by people who have the mistaken belief that these are weight-loss techniques. (They're not.) Misusing these drugs (or others) is dangerous and unhealthy and may be an indication that a person has, or is in the process of developing, an eating disorder.

Remember: Drugs (including herbal and over-the-counter drugs) taken by kids and teens should only be used under the supervision of a parent or health care professional.

ALL EATING DISORDERS REQUIRE TREATMENT—ALL OF THEM

Concerned about a friend? Talk to her or his parent, your parent—or another trusted adult—about the situation.

Friendship means watching out for one another. This includes getting help from a trusted adult when you think your friend has a problem.

QUESTIONS?

Reliable information about eating disorders is available from:

National Eating Disorders Association

603 Stewart Street, Suite 803

Seattle, WA 98101

Phone: (206) 382-3587

Fax: (206) 829-8501

http://www.NationalEatingDisorders.org

National Institute of Mental Health

Office of Communications and Public Liaison

Public inquiries, phone: (301) 443-4513

E-mail: nimhinfo@nih.gov

Web site: http://www.nimh.nih.gov

Or try contacting your local county health department, listed in the front of the phone book under "government listings."

YOU ARE CARED ABOUT

When you need help, please reach out to a trustworthy, reliable adult—like an adult family member or friend, health care professional, teacher, school administrator, public safety officer (like a police officer or firefighter), or any other responsible adult you think can help you. In an emergency, call 911 or the police emergency number for your area.

HOTLINES

Hotlines are telephone numbers you can call when you need help with a problem. The very first pages of the phone book usually list hotline numbers along with other emergency numbers. The information operator (411) or regular operator (0) also can help get hotline numbers.

The Boys and Girls Town National Hotline is set up to help kids in crisis.

This organization is staffed by trained volunteers who can help callers identify their problems, explore options, and develop a plan of action. They also offer referrals to community-based services, support groups, and even shelters if necessary.

Boys and Girls Town National Hotline: The call is free—and it's available twenty-four hours a day, seven days a week.

1 (800) 448-3000, United States & Canada

Hearing impaired?

1 (800) 448-1833 (TTY)

Help is out there—it's just a phone call away.

chapter 17

BEGIN BY BEGINNING

Would you like to get on track—or back on track? Here's a tip list:

QUICK START

Beginning tomorrow, or as soon as possible, eat a nutritious breakfast, lunch, and dinner—and two healthy snacks in between. Review The Cactus Plan (chapter 5) regarding recommendations for healthy eating.

☺ Focus on eating a total of at least seven servings of rainbow-colored fruits and vegetables (combined).

☺ Drink fluids throughout the day, including water. Drink about six to eight cups, total—and, of course, not all at once!

☺ The next time you buy milk, make yours 1 percent low-fat or skim.

☺ The next time you buy bread, make yours (enriched) whole grain.

☺ The next time you buy breakfast cereal, make yours (enriched) whole grain—with whole grains at the top of the ingredients list printed on the box.

☺ Sleep for eight hours tonight and every night you can.

☺ Enjoy a little sunshine.

☺ Schedule some quality time with a parent in the very near future. In this case, quality time would mean together time—when you can have the opportunity to talk and listen to each other. Maybe it could involve taking a walk, playing a game, preparing a meal.

☺ Set reasonable goals for yourself involving safe, supervised, fun physical activity. Review The Cactus Plan regarding recommendations for routine physical activity.

☺ Keep track. Are you reaching your goals?

☺ Make a list of physical activities that you like or you think you'd like to try out if there's an opportunity. Ask your parent to help you find out where there are safe, supervised physical activity programs/classes for kids and/or families in your community. Schedule a time for you and your parent to call around, visit the facilities, and get information. Sign up for something that sounds good and go for it!

☺ Do you have enough options for varied, enjoyable physical activity at school? Think about specific PE and after-school programs that could be added to your school programs. What would really be a blast? Make a list. Talk to friends. Think about a responsible adult associated with your school who might advise you and your friends on how to get the ball rolling.

☺ Take an informal survey on what foods, including snacks and drinks, are available in your school. Check out the vending machines. Can you think of ways choices can be improved? Jot down your ideas. Begin to think about which friends, teachers, parents, and/or school administrators you might ask to join forces with you to help initiate positive changes.

☺ Challenge yourself. Begin viewing ads more critically. Try to figure out what is being marketed to you, how it's being marketed, and why. Ask yourself: Do I really need this? Is this good for me?

☺ For the next few days, write down each TV program you watch and how long you watch it. Also, log time spent at the computer or playing video games. Total it up at bedtime each night. Then take some time to sit down and review your notes. Figure out where you can make some cuts in screen time with your ultimate viewing goal being not more than two hours a day.

☺ Reassure yourself. You can be healthy, strong, and prepared to meet life's challenges.

☺ Set goals. Make plans. Keep track of your progress.

You can do this.

YOU CAN.

VITAMIN CHART

Want to know what vitamins do for you?

VITAMIN A

Needed for:

Immune functions (fighting infection and disease), healthy eyes, growth and repair of cells and tissues (skin, hair, organs), protecting cells from damage (antioxidant)

Some sources:

Eggs, carrots, sweet potatoes, kale, spinach, fruits, low-fat fortified dairy products

VITAMIN C

Needed for:

Protecting cells from damage (antioxidant), wound healing, strong blood vessels, healthy gums and skin

Some sources:

Oranges, grapefruit, tangerines, berries, melons, broccoli, green and red peppers, tomatoes

VITAMIN D

Needed for:

Bone and teeth formation

Some sources:

Egg yolk, salmon, fatty fish, vitamin-D-fortified milk; also made in skin exposed to sunlight

VITAMIN E

Needed for:

Protecting cells from damage (antioxidant)

Some sources:

Corn oil, seed oils, milk, wheat germ, nuts, dark green vegetables, whole grains, beans

VITAMIN K

Needed for:

Formation of blood-clotting agents and bone formation

Some sources:

Green leafy vegetables, cereal, milk, egg yolk, sardines, broccoli, cabbage, kale, turnip greens

VITAMIN B-1 (THIAMINE)

Needed for:

Carb metabolism, maintaining appetite, nerve function, growth, and muscle tone

Some sources:

Wheat germ, pork, whole and enriched grains, legumes, nuts, seafood

VITAMIN B-2 (RIBOFLAVIN)

Needed for:

Carb, protein, and fat metabolism; healthy eyes, skin, and nerves

Some sources:

Low-fat milk products, green leafy vegetables, whole and enriched grains, eggs

VITAMIN B-3 (NIACIN)

Needed for:

Carb, protein, and fat metabolism; health of digestive system; blood circulation; nerve function; appetite; healthy skin

Some sources:

Poultry, fish, eggs, whole and enriched grains, dried beans and peas

VITAMIN B-6 (PYRIDOXINE)

Needed for:

Carb and protein metabolism, formation of

antibodies, red blood cells, nerve function

Some sources:

Fish, poultry, nuts, soybeans, whole grains, eggs

VITAMIN B-12

Needed for:

Carb, protein, and fat metabolism; maintaining nervous system; blood formation

Some sources:

Fish, poultry, eggs, 1 percent low-fat and skim milk, vitamin-B-12-fortified soy products

BIOTIN

Needed for:

Carb, protein, and fat metabolism

Some sources:

Egg yolk, meat, 1 percent low-fat and skim milk, dark green vegetables; also made by microorganisms in intestinal tract

FOLIC ACID

Needed for:

Red blood cell and other cell formation, protein metabolism

Some sources:

Green leafy vegetables, dried beans, poultry, enriched grain products, oranges (and orange juice), nuts, kale, spinach, yeast, soybeans, wheat germ

PANTOTHENIC ACID

Needed for:

Conversion of food into energy, vitamin utilization, nerve function

Some sources:

Most plant and animal foods, especially lean meats, whole grains, legumes

MINERAL CHART

And here's what certain minerals do for you:

CALCIUM

Needed for:

Bone and teeth formation; regulation of heartbeat, muscle action, and nerve function; blood clotting

Some sources:

Foods containing low-fat (or nonfat) milk— 1 percent low-fat and skim milk, low-fat cheese, yogurt, cottage cheese—and broccoli, calcium-fortified orange juice, calcium-fortified soy milk, calcium-fortified rice milk, salmon with bones, green leafy vegetables

IRON

Needed for:

Formation of hemoglobin in blood (and myoglobin in muscle), which supplies oxygen to cells

Some sources:

Fish, shellfish, poultry, lean meat, beans, whole and enriched grains, green leafy vegetables, liver

POTASSIUM

Needed for:

Fluid balance, controlling activity of heart muscles, nervous system

Some sources:

Bananas, oranges, apricots, avocados, potatoes, bran, peanuts, legumes, lean meat, low-fat milk products

ZINC

Needed for:

Growth, taste and smell sensitivity, immune function, wound healing

Some sources:

Oysters, legumes, lean meat, liver, eggs, seafood, whole grains, low-fat milk products

IODINE

Needed for:

Function of thyroid gland, which controls metabolism

Some sources:

Seafood, iodized salt

CHROMIUM

Needed for:

Glucose and fat metabolism to energy, increasing effectiveness of insulin, muscle function

Some sources:

Cheese, whole grains, lean meat, peas, beans, wheat germ

COPPER

Needed for:

Formation of red blood cells, skin, and connective tissues

Some sources:

Nuts, seeds, seafood, oysters, cocoa powder

MAGNESIUM

Needed for:

Food metabolism, nerve and muscle function, bone growth

Some sources:

Nuts, green vegetables, whole grains, beans

MANGANESE

Needed for:

Bone growth and development, sex hormone production, cell formation

Some sources:

Nuts, whole grains, vegetables, fruits, tea, coffee, bran

SELENIUM

Needed for:

Protecting cells from damage (antioxidant), healthy heart muscle

Some sources:

Seafood, whole grains, seeds

SHOPPING LIST

(okay to copy this)

THE CACTUS PLAN SHOPPING GUIDELINES

FLUIDS (ALSO NOTED BELOW)

100 percent fruit juice

100 percent vegetable juice

Tomato juice

1 percent low-fat or skim milk

Calcium-fortified soy milk

Calcium-fortified rice milk

Bottled water with 100 percent fruit juice added

Soups (low sodium)

Mineral water/bottled water

Fruits, vegetables, salsa

Others:

WHOLE GRAINS

Bagels (whole grain)

Barley

Bread—whole grain, enriched

Bulgur

Breakfast cereals—whole grain, enriched

Chips, whole grain (fried in unhydrogenated plant oil or baked)

Crackers, whole grain (without hydrogenated oils)

Couscous

Cooked cereals—whole grain, enriched

Flour, stone-ground

Oatmeal

Whole wheat pasta

Whole wheat pita bread

Popcorn kernels

Rice, brown/enriched

Brown rice cakes

Multigrain rolls

Whole wheat tortillas

Soups containing whole grains (barley, brown rice, etc.)

Others:

VEGETABLES: THINK RED, YELLOW, ORANGE, BLUE, GREEN, WHITE

Fresh

Canned

Frozen

Jarred (beets)

Juice (in cartons, bottled, canned)

Also:

Salsa

Tomato sauce

Spaghetti sauce (low sodium)

Soups with vegetables in them (low sodium)

Others:

PLANT OILS

Canola oil

Olive oil

Peanut oil

Soybean oil

Corn oil

Salad dressings made with the above oils

Soft tub margarine

Others:

FRUITS: THINK RED, YELLOW, PINK, ORANGE, BLUE, GREEN, WHITE

Fresh

Canned

Frozen

Dried

Jarred (applesauce)

Juice (in cartons, bottled, canned)

Calcium-fortified juices

Frozen juice bars

Sorbet

Fruit ices

Others:

NUTS, BEANS (AND OTHER LEGUMES), AND SOY PROTEIN FOODS

Canned beans

Dried beans

Dried lentils

Seeds

Nuts

Peanut/almond/soy butter (look for those that are made without hydrogenated oils)

Hummus

Tofu (produce/dairy section)

Tempeh

Soups with beans and lentils in them (low sodium)

Others:

LOW-FAT MILK, LOW-FAT YOGURT, LOW-FAT CHEESE, LOW-FAT DAIRY

Reduced fat, partially skim, and skim milk cheese

Low-fat cottage cheese

Low-fat cream cheese

Low-fat cheese dips and spreads

1 percent low-fat or skim milk

Low-fat sour cream

Low-fat yogurt

Non-fat dry milk

Frozen low-fat yogurt

Soups (low sodium) with low-fat milk in them

Others:

POULTRY, EGGS, FISH, SEAFOOD, LEAN RED MEAT

Eggs

Chicken

Tuna

Turkey

Ground turkey

Salmon

Sardines

Shellfish

Fish

Lean red meat

Beef: eye of round, top sirloin, extra-lean ground beef, tenderloin

Pork: tenderloin, sirloin, top loin

Lamb: leg shank

Luncheon meats: 95 to 99 percent fat free

Canned fish, poultry, seafood, meat

Cooked, sliced, packaged deli poultry and meat

Soups with poultry, fish, seafood, lean red meat in them (low sodium)

Others:

CONDIMENTS AND SAUCES

Hot sauce

Jams

Jellies

Mayo, low fat

Mustard

Relish

Honey

Maple syrup

Molasses

Salad dressings

Soy sauce

Olives

Peppers

Others:

HERBS AND SPICES

Basil

Cilantro

Ginger

Parsley

Rosemary

Sage

Others:

HOUSEHOLD SUPPLIES

Pet food and supplies

Paper napkins, paper towels, paper bags

Plastic bags for snacks, food storage, trash

Fluoridated toothpaste (dental floss/toothbrush)

Hand/face soap

Lotion

Shampoo, conditioner

Others:

INDEX

as food group, 33, 68
shopping for, 66–67, 113
fruit juice, 31, 67

Girls and Boys Town National Hotline, 107
glucose, 12
grains, 7, 32
as food group, 69–70
refined, 8
whole, 7, 32, 67, 112–13
growth and, growth spurt, 2, 43, 15–18

heart, 22–24
height, 43
hemoglobin, 17, 18
herbal medicines and supplements, 19
herbs, 114
hotlines, 107
household supplies, 114
hydrogenated fats, 23, 40

ice cream, 36
insoluble fiber, 6
Internet, health information on, 19–21, 57, 63, 75, 89, 92
iodine, 112
iron, 17–18, 74, 111
deficiency in, 17, 18
overdose of, 14
sources of, 18
in vegetarian diet, 55–56

key words, in food shopping, 67–68

labels, food, 13, 72–75, 74
lactase, 16, 17
lactose intolerance, 16–17, 27–28
lean meats, 27, 36–37, 114
leftovers, food safety and, 58, 62
legumes, 70, 113
lentils, 35
liver, cholesterol produced in, 24
low-fat:
dairy foods, 35, 71, 113–14
dietary emphasis on, 68, 71
low-impact activity, 90
lungs, 22

macronutrients, 11
magazines, portrayal of women in, 98–100
magnesium, 112
manganese, 112
margarine, 23
marketing, to young people, 98–100
meat, red, 6, 18, 37, 114
media literacy, 97–98
melanoma, 10

menopause, 17
menstruation, 17
metabolism, 1–2, 26
micronutrients, 13–18
milk, 6
low-fat and skim, 12, 31, 41, 42
rice, 42
soy, 15, 42, 55
minerals, 2, 15–18, 111–12
minimally processed foods, 40
monosodium glutamate (MSG), 19
muscle mass, 13

National Academy of Sciences, 13
National Eating Disorders Association, 106
National Institute of Mental Health, 106
niacin, 110
nutrients, 1, 11–14
nutritional supplements, 14, 16, 19, 35, 55, 56, 114
nutrition facts, 74
nutritionists, 21
nuts, 2, 7, 35, 70, 113

obesity, 76
oils:
hydrogenated, 23, 40, 68, 73
from plants, 8, 34, 70, 113
orange juice, calcium-fortified, 41, 42
"organic," on food label, 67
ovaries, 17
overexercising, 89
oxalic acid, 55
oxygen, 22
aerobic exercise and, 89
in blood, 17, 18

palm oil, 23
pantothenic acid, 111
parasites, 58
parents, communication with, 102–4
partially hydrogenated oil, 23, 40, 68, 73
pasta, 70
pectin, 6
perishable foods, 64–65
physical activity, 3, 9, 28, 76–83, 86–93
fluid replacement and, 9, 88
safety tips for, 87, 88, 91
stretches for, 84–85
phytochemicals, 7, 27
phytonutrients, 35
plant oils, 8, 34, 70, 113
Poison Control Hotline, 14
poisoning, in children, 14
popcorn, 36
portions, see serving sizes
posture, 3

Lilian Cheung and Mavis Jukes became close friends while working together on **Be Healthy! It's a Girl Thing: Food, Fitness, and Feeling Great.**

LILIAN CHEUNG is a doctor of science in nutrition and a registered dietitian. She is the Director of Health Promotion and Communications and a lecturer in the Department of Nutrition at the Harvard School of Public Health.

Lilian Cheung has committed her professional life to raising awareness of the importance of combining nutrition and physical activity to promote health in young people. She championed the creation of the school-based program Eat Well and Keep Moving, an interdisciplinary curriculum for teaching nutrition and physical activity.

She has advised national media outlets (magazines, newspapers, and television) and government agencies, including the National Cancer Institute and the Centers for Disease Control and Prevention. She has also served as an executive director of a private practice in nutritional counseling and as a nutritional consultant to the Boston Ballet School.

MAVIS JUKES has twenty years of writing experience and ten years of teaching experience, and is a member of the California Bar.

She has written many books for kids and teens, including three other health-related titles: *It's a Girl Thing: How to Stay Healthy, Safe, and in Charge* (for girls 12 and up); *Growing Up: It's a Girl Thing: Straight Talk About First Bras, First Periods, and Your Changing Body* (for girls 8 and up); and *The Guy Book: An Owner's Manual: Maintenance, Safety, and Operating Instructions for Teens* (for boys 13 and up).